Closing the Writing Gap

Writing is a fundamental part of our daily lives. From writing emails to preparing job applications, writing filters into our working lives and is essential in every exam and school assessment. Though seemingly 'natural', writing proves devilishly difficult for far too many school pupils and this can have a lasting impact on their academic and life success. To close this gap, we need to ensure that every teacher has the knowledge and skill to teach writing with confidence.

In *Closing the Writing Gap,* Alex Quigley makes sense of the history and 'science' of writing, synthesising the debates and presenting a wealth of useable evidence about how children develop most efficiently as successful writers. Offering practical strategies for teachers at every stage of their teaching career, the book helps teachers to be experts in how pupils learn to write, from the big picture of planning, editing and revising their writing, to the vital importance of grammar and spelling with accuracy.

This essential book presents the case for teacher-led efforts to develop pupils' writing and provides practical solutions for teachers across the curriculum, incorporating easy-to-use tools, resources, and classroom activities.

Alex Quigley is a National Content Manager at the national educational charity, the Education Endowment Foundation, UK. Previously, he was Director of Huntington Research School and an English teacher at Huntington School, York. He is also a columnist for TES and Teach Secondary.

"'Our lives can be filled and fulfilled by writing', says Alex Quigley. In this important new book: 'That story begins with our birth certificate and ends with our epitaph ...'. I can't think of a text which better articulates the importance of writing, and then goes on to articulate how to put ambition into practice. It is a book of wise principles and practical implementation. In it, Quigley establishes himself even further as my go-to source of insights into the all-important subject of whole-school literacy."

Geoff Barton, General Secretary, Association of School and College Leaders, and former English teacher

"This book provides an easy-to-read and entertaining synthesis of research on writing, beginning with a compelling overview of how writing developed. It has written text at its heart and offers readers a succinct insight into textual research and its practical application to the writing classroom. The book is a rich source of directions for further reading and examples of strategies for teaching writing which will support teachers to reflect on what happens in their writing classrooms and to make enabling changes."

Professor Debra Myhill, Director of the Centre for Research in Writing, University of Exeter, UK

"Alex Quigley has written another brilliant book for classroom teachers and school leaders. This book gets right to the heart of closing the writing gap; it is thought provoking for the reflective teacher whilst also offering helpful guidance and advice for every teacher. Alex is an exceptional writer himself, communicating his expertise and experiences with clarity and precision."

Kate Jones, History teacher, education consultant, author, and blogger @KateJones_Teach

"As this important and necessary book makes clear, many teachers struggle with the teaching of writing. Teachers recognise the huge significance of writing, but they find it difficult to translate their own writing expertise for the benefit of their students. In *Closing the Writing Gap* Alex Quigley provides evidence-informed, highly practical strategies to bridge this pedagogical chasm. Both erudite and accessible, it covers the vital ingredients of effective writing teaching – from the building blocks of the grammar to the art of rhetoric and the pragmatics of the drafting and editing process. *Closing the Writing Gap* is an essential addition to the bookshelves of all teachers."

Mark Roberts, English teacher and author of *The Boy Question*

"*Closing the Writing Gap* is the perfect antidote to the problems surrounding writing in the classroom today. Alex Quigley's razor-sharp focus pinpoints the clear ways teachers can address and improve writing in the classroom. The book's real strength, for me, is its practical approach to writing, offering strategies and methods that all teachers could, and should, use in the classroom. Alex walks you through the various aspects of writing and provides a brilliant insight into how practitioners can support and improve writing in their classroom today. The book to read if you want to improve disciplinary literacy in a school."

Chris Curtis, Head of English and author of *How to Teach English*

Closing the Writing Gap

Alex Quigley

LONDON AND NEW YORK

Cover image: © Pixhall/Alamy Stock Photo

First published 2022
by Routledge
4 Park Square, Milton Park, Abingdon, Oxon OX14 4RN

and by Routledge
605 Third Avenue, New York, NY 10158

Routledge is an imprint of the Taylor & Francis Group, an informa business

British Library Cataloguing-in-Publication Data
A catalogue record for this book is available from the British Library

Library of Congress Cataloging-in-Publication Data
A catalog record has been requested for this book

ISBN: 978-1-032-01767-9 (hbk)
ISBN: 978-1-032-01771-6 (pbk)
ISBN: 978-1-003-17996-2 (ebk)

DOI: 10.4324/9781003179962

Typeset in Celeste and Optima
by Newgen Publishing UK

To Mum and Dad, for giving me everything I needed to write my own story.

To Katy, Freya, and Noah, for making your indelible mark on me.

Contents

Acknowledgements

My sincere thanks go to Katy Gilbert, Phil Stock, Caroline Bilton, Marcus Jones, David Didau, and John Tomsett, for offering essential insights and edits that have informed chapters in this book.

Thank you to Molly and Annamarie, along with the team at Routledge, for their sustained support and expertise.

I would like to acknowledge and thank the many researchers, and writers, who have developed the field of research and thinking attending the teaching of writing. The influential experts who inform this book include Debra Myhill, David Crystal, Steve Graham, Pie Corbett, Judith Hochman and Natalie Wexler, Karen Harris, and many more. They have immeasurably influenced my thinking and the writing of this book and I hope my bibliography steers people to the best of insights on teaching writing.

Finally, thank you to the teachers and school leaders, whose schools I have visited and work closely with, who have informed the ideas in this book. Alongside a brilliant array of teachers, my EEF colleagues have supported my thinking, such as writing about literacy in secondary schools with Robbie Coleman, hearing about 'Grammar time' from Iggy Rhodes, and working on literacy with Caroline Bilton, and more.

Note: All pupils named in this book have pseudonyms and adapted characteristics to protect their identity.

1 Introduction

Our lives can be filled and fulfilled by writing. That story begins with our birth certificate and ends with our epitaph. In between, each day, we use writing to learn, to love, to remember, to console, to entertain, to imagine, to argue, and to simply *be*.

These blots of ink you see before you embody the greatest tool of our modern civilisation. They represent our urge to communicate and our means to do so. In a mere few thousand years, we have gone from a small number of people engraving notches on stone and bone to around five billion people being able to write and to communicate. The story of writing has rapidly accelerated, with writing quickly becoming an act of near-instant global connectedness.

Though most of the world now enjoys the power and pleasure of writing, there remains a gap between those who can write with fluency and skill and those who cannot. Around 7.1 million adults in England are functionally illiterate.[1] Put simply, imagine lacking the confidence to email your boss or to write a job application. Too many adults and young people are unable to perform these seemingly simple acts of daily writing, or to enjoy the potential

DOI: 10.4324/9781003179962-1

benefits they offer. That is the harsh truth of being functionally illiterate.

No statistic, however big, nor school data, can capture the frustration and daily losses suffered by those people, and pupils, who struggle to write.

Sadly, most young people and adults who struggle to write do not go on to write the story of their own lives and their voices go unheard. Instead, debates about writing get embroiled in narrow grumblings about grammar terminology or squabbles about style. Meanwhile, too many pupils suffer countless small losses and teachers lack training in the fundamentals of teaching writing, grammar, and more. The sound and fury of media headlines seldom translates into support for teachers to close this writing gap.

The dubious lore that 'we all have a novel within us' belies a cold truth. Few people write a novel. Even fewer still write daily with the confidence and fluency that those who have flourished at school can take for granted. We labour under the miscomprehension that writing is a natural gift and is not hard-earned. Too easily, we forget the thousands of hours of deliberate practice it takes to learn to write, from the mark making of young children with crayons, or similar, to pupils gripped by the pressure of writing extended essays in vast exam halls.

It is argued that writing is the 'neglected "R"'[2] in comparison to reading and a(r)ithmetic. Given that writing ability will either unleash or circumscribe the talents of our pupils, we need to give writing the attention it deserves, in every classroom, at every stage of schooling.

The writing gap in the classroom

Let's begin with a writing activity, just like those undertaken by pupils daily.

First, quickly read this short passage about a cyclone in Kolkata:

> A powerful and catastrophic tropical cyclone has hit the east Indian city of Kolkata. The devastating storm has led to the tragic deaths of an estimated one hundred people in West Bengal and beyond. Cyclone Amphan destroyed coastal areas with a storm surge of around sixteen feet, triggering widespread flooding. As a result, low-lying areas have been left in swamp-like conditions, with houses flattened, power outages, and thousands of trees uprooted in the wake of the cyclone.

Now, your classroom writing task is to write a single sentence summary, in ten words or less, of this passage about cyclone Amphan in the box below. And, crucially, you must write the summary sentence with your non-writing hand.

How did you do? Just as importantly: how did this task make you *feel*?

Take a moment to consider the sheer array of knowledge and skill that meant you were able to enact this essential, and perennial, writing activity.

On reflection, you will have noted the physical discomfort of writing with your 'other' hand. It reminds us of the hard-won nature of automatic, fluent handwriting. For pupils, these basic writing processes can help or hinder writing goals. Second, to write a short summary, you had to bring to bear an array of reading knowledge and skill. You likely skimmed and scanned the words describing Kolkata, activating lots of essential background knowledge, before considering how to filter the essential information into a few words. Then, understanding intuitively the nature of a clear and complete sentence, you summarised your reading with a rapid distillation into your own words.

When we consider the dizzying array of moves writers make in a matter of moments, we recognise the difficulty faced by so many novice pupils when they are expected to write in the classroom. You may not be functionally illiterate by any measure, but you can still find this task tricky, just as pupils can find writing in the classroom difficult. And so, the subtle, near hidden 'writing gap' exists and persists in these countless daily writing tasks for our pupils.

It is no surprise then that the complex act of writing is described as tantamount to a game of chess.[3] For most writing tasks in the classroom, a pupil will be thinking about their many 'moves': handwriting, word choices, spelling, paragraphing, writing for their audience, activating their prior knowledge, along with considering the purpose and genre of their writing, and more.

Take some time to consider the experience of a sixteen-year-old pupil sitting something like twenty lengthy examinations. Each time they play on a different chess board, in rapid succession, with a different opponent, but in each exam, there is the relentless demand to make their writing moves with speed, skill, and confidence.

Not only is an array of complex moves enacted during all acts of writing, in the typical school day, pupils are expected to undertake many different *types* of writing.

Though many instances of pupils' writing are in the form of short answers to questions[4] – or note-making, for older pupils in particular – any given school day can include a range of writing types and teacher approaches, from a story or an essay to a short exam answer.

Consider the moving target of writing at different phases and key stages. In year 2, a pupil could be expected to write an imagined account of the Great Fire of London, quickly followed by a written record of science experiments on materials burning. Fast forward to year 9, with pupils moving from note-taking in science, to essay writing in history, then onto annotation in art, and finally some narrative writing in English. Each act of writing proves subtly different, with different generic features and stylistic devices, along with often radically different approaches to how that writing is taught, planned, drafted, edited, and revised.

Given we can recognise, with some intuition, how to write strong sentences, stories, and more, without a deep understanding of the process, we can be prone to take the teaching of writing for granted. It can mistakenly be viewed as something to be acquired naturally, just like talk. Though reading, or physics, or algebraic equations, may prove hard for pupils of all ages and stages to master, it has been argued that the ability of our pupils to translate their thoughts into writing may be the hardest skill of all to develop.[5]

Teachers observe the difficulties faced by pupils who struggle with writing each day. When writing falters, it offers one of the more visible and tangible ways to understand how well our pupils are, or are not, learning. We observe common pitfalls, such as spelling errors, grammatical slips, arguments without evidence, extended writing that lacks organisation, ideas and impact, and much more.

Concerns about the writing development of pupils occur the world over.[6] And yet, though a mass of useful practices and research evidence exists, teachers can miss the opportunity to teach pupils critical writing processes, such as planning and revising their writing for success.[7]

In practical terms, pupils are often not expected to write more complex texts longer than a paragraph.[8] As such, the chess match shrinks to shifting some pawns without too much forethought. Shortened writing can go unstructured, so even the conscious crafting and modelling of sentences can prove uncommon. In narrowing writing across the school curriculum to a succession of short answers, often with exams in mind, we miss the countless opportunities offered by writing to enhance our pupils' understanding of what they read and hear in the classroom.[9]

The messy, complex, rich and rewarding act of writing can and should be at the heart of best practice in the classroom. The demands of extended academic writing – or 'school writing' – can be met over time, and we can close the writing gap, one move at a time.

The teacher writing gap

I am haunted by the ghosts of my teaching past.

Daniel is one such ghost. He was a kind and hardworking young man. Years later, I can still remember his handwriting. His blue biro would press hard against the paper, drumming out his commitment to write well deep into every page. And yet, his earnest, tight-lettered handwriting could not mask his writing struggles, his misspellings, or his missteps.

If it was an essay on Shakespeare, or narrative writing of his own, Daniel would write more and more. With more writing came more mistakes. Despite racing through pages and pages of writing, he would continue to crash into a glass ceiling of awkward expression, limited vocabulary, and gaps in his knowledge. I would daub his writing with feedback and undertake a vocabulary exercise here or there, or try to instruct a common sentence flaw or two, but the hard truth was Daniel's knowledge of how to write skilfully was insufficient and, crucially, so was mine.

It started with my schooling. I was part of a generation of schoolchildren who were not taught grammar. It was deemed 'a waste of time'[10] and 'worth ignoring'[11] by educationalists. As a result, a gap in grammar knowledge has compromised the teaching of writing and language for a long time.

In my teacher training, the teaching of writing was limited to offering up some engaging stimulus, a few writing moves to perform as tricks, and some static planning templates. Describing a sherbet lemon (not subordinate clauses) was deemed the height of creative writing in the secondary English classroom in those heady days. For pupils like Daniel, dishing out sherbet lemons and expecting effective writing was always going to turn sour. Though my insufficient teaching wasn't the only cause, it was predictable that many of Daniel's GCSE grades would be compromised by his writing weaknesses.

As a former teacher of English – with the overt expectation of expertise in the teaching of writing – it is an embarrassing admission. And yet, I am not alone. Countless teachers feel ill-equipped to teach struggling writers, or to teach the artful craft of sentence construction across a range of key stages, subjects, and schools.[12]

The many constructive choices that can emerge from teaching grammar embedded in writing can be squandered through a lack of knowledge of how to grapple with grammar in the act of writing.[13] Beyond a knowledge of grammar and its role in writing, why might teachers miss the many small but significant opportunities to systematically improve the writing of pupils? The answer is likely that teachers do not teach in this way because they do not have the confidence to do so.

Teachers too often lack vital training in how to teach writing successfully. This chastening experience is mirrored in the writing of Colin Peacock:

> Many teachers of writing, probably, begin their careers, as I did, with a body of largely untested beliefs and limited professional skills and have in the main to learn as best they can from the successes they achieve in the classroom and the mistakes they make.
>
> *Teaching Writing: A Systematic Approach,* by Colin Peacock[14]

How many teachers reading this book, at all key stages, can relate to this problematic assessment of teacher preparation?

Lots of pupils experience few difficulties with writing, regardless of the preparedness of their teacher. They are typically the same pupils who read habitually and come from homes where a literate environment of bookshelves and easy access to technology is the norm. They may intuitively grasp the subtle differences in genres and subject-specific writing. When they write a sentence in a scientific report, they use apt specialised vocabulary, an impassive tone, and carefully crafted clauses. They *get* academic writing, whether they label it as such or not.

Writing can seem so easy for some pupils, but this can deceive us into thinking that *all* pupils naturally make the equivalent writing gains over time.

As Peacock shares, 'Some children do learn to write by simply writing but likely a small proportion.' Pupils like Daniel, even if they commit to try, don't absorb the textbook explanations of sentence structures or the dictionary definition of rare grammatical terms with ease, nor do they make sense of the expert 'mentor text' displayed to them as a model of excellence. When Daniel was expected to bring all the complex chess moves of an expert writer together in the exam hall, his failure to play the game successfully was brutally exposed.

Let's linger on the committed efforts of Daniel, along with the thousands and thousands of pupils just like him who suffer small daily losses when they attempt to write in the classroom.

It is not good enough to leave teachers unconfident and untaught when it comes to writing instruction.

I am left thinking about Daniel and where he is now. I wonder how many frustrations could have been avoided, or how many additional opportunities could have been gifted to him if he had possessed the powers of a skilled writer.

The imperative to improve writing

Most teachers explain their imperative to teach emerged very close to home. It may have been a parent or grandparent who was a teacher. For me, one source of motivation to teach was having a parent who had not acquired the skill to write with confidence at school and seeing how that had limited their choices in life.

What every teacher understands is that when pupils possess the crucial skills of writing and reading they are empowered to make more choices. Indeed, the very act of writing is a 'huge network of interrelated choices'.[15] Each word and each sentence can prove a careful crafting of voice and an exercise of choice for developing writers.

When you can write well, you can choose to apply for that essential qualification, or to write that dream job application. When you write well, you can choose to pen a political speech, or to bare your heart in a message to a hoped-for sweetheart.

We can romanticise a little about the power of expression that is unlocked by the ability to write well. In doing so, we should not be distracted from the recognition that skilled academic writing, everything from single sentences to extended essays, requires rigorous explicit instruction.

There is no easy 'silver bullet' to improving the writing of pupils in all corners of the curriculum. Alas, the sage words of advice from professional writers will often prove contradictory. As the writer William Somerset Maugham put it: 'There are three rules for writing the novel. Unfortunately, no one knows what they are.' Equally, the wisdom of great poets will not usefully inform pupils how to write a 6-mark answer, under time pressure, in an A level biology exam.

Though there are not three simple rules for all writing development, there are evidence-informed steps every teacher, and school, can take to support the development of writing and to close the writing gap. Here are my seven suggested steps that inform the rest of this book:

1. Train teachers in the art and science of writing.
2. Take advantage of talk and the rhetorical roots of writing.
3. Explicitly teach and model the stages of the writing process.
4. Offer pupils the gift of grammar, so that they can make informed writing choices.
5. Concentrate on crafting great sentences.
6. Prioritise disciplinary writing.
7. Plan for focused feedback and assess writing excellence.

The imperative for better writing instruction, with these seven steps, is the increased chance of school success for every pupil in our care. When the teaching of writing improves, it is helpful for every pupil, but for pupils like Daniel, it is likely to matter even more.

IN SHORT ...

- Millions of adults leave school struggling to write. It is a gap that can start early, persist throughout school, and prove a limiting factor for school success.
- The sheer array of writing moves that are enacted every time pupils are expected to write in the classroom is tantamount to playing a game of chess.
- We need to attend to the teacher 'writing gap' and a lack of knowledge and confidence in how to teach writing. Teachers need to be supported with training, tools, and time.
- Every act of writing is a 'huge, interrelated network of choices'. We need to ensure that our pupils are empowered to make the best choices when it comes to their writing.

Notes

1 Kuczera, M., Field, S., & Windisch, H. C. (2012). Building skills for all: A review of England. OECD. Retrieved from: www.oecd.org/education/skills-beyond-school/building-skills-for-all-review-of-england.pdf.

2 Magrath, C. P. et al. (2014). The neglected 'R': The need for a writing revolution. The National Commission on Writing in America's Schools and Colleges. Retrieved from: https://archive.nwp.org/cs/public/download/nwp_file/21478/the-neglected-r-college-board-nwp-report.pdf?x-r=pcfile_d.

3 Kellogg, R. (2008). Training writing skills: A cognitive developmental perspective. *Journal of Writing Research*, *1*(1), pp.1–26. doi:10.17239/jowr-2008.01.01.1.

4 Applebee, A. N., Langer, J. A., Nystrand, M., & Gamoran, A. (2003). Discussion-based approaches to developing understanding: Classroom instruction and student performance in middle and high school English. *American Educational Research Journal, 40*(3), 685–730.

5 Graham, S., MacArthur, C. A., & Hebert, M. (2019). *Best Practices in Writing Instruction.* London: The Guilford Press.

6 Graham, S., & Rijlaarsdam, G. (2016). Writing education around the globe: Introduction and call for a new global analysis. *Reading and Writing, 29,* 781–792.

7 Dockrell, J. E., Marshall, C. R., & Wyse, D. (2016). Teachers' reported practices for teaching writing in England. *Reading and Writing, 29,* 409–434. doi:10.1007/s11145-015-9605-9.

8 Gilbert, J., & Graham, S. (2010). Teaching writing to elementary students in grades 4–6: A national survey. *The Elementary School Journal, 110,* 494–518.

9 Graham, S., & Hebert, M. A. (2010). *Writing to read: Evidence for how writing can improve reading. A Carnegie Corporation Time to Act Report.* Washington, DC: Alliance for Excellent Education.

10 Muller, H. J. (1967). *The uses of English: Guidelines for the teaching of English from the Anglo-American Conference at Dartmouth College.* New York: Holt, Rinehart and Winston.

11 Elbow, P. (1981). *Writing with power: Techniques for mastering the writing process.* New York: Oxford University Press.

12 Brindle, M., Graham, S., Harris, K. R., & Hebert, M. (2012). Third and fourth grade teacher's classroom practices in writing: A national survey. *Reading and Writing, 29*(5).

13 Myhill, D., Jones, S., & Watson, A. (2012). Grammar matters: How teachers' grammatical knowledge impacts on the teaching of writing. *Teaching and Teacher Education, 36,* 77–91.

14 Peacock, C. (2019). *Teaching writing: A systematic approach.* Oxon: Routledge.

15 Halliday, M. A. K. (2003). Introduction: On the 'architecture' of human language. In Jonathan Webster (Ed.), *On language and linguistics.* (Volume 3 in the Collected Works of M. A. K. Halliday). London and New York: Continuum.

2 A history of writing

The wise aphorism goes that 'Those who cannot remember the past are condemned to repeat it.'[1] When it comes to the history of writing, every teacher can learn from the lessons of the past and they may even benefit from repeating some of it.

The story of writing is 'a tale of adventure which spans some twenty thousand years and touches every aspect of human life.'[2] Indeed, the history of writing is tantamount to the history of modern civilisation. The development of language – first speech, before it was then enshrined in writing – has been the means to help drive civilised progress, whilst providing a record of how those civilisations survived and thrived.

From the invention of the alphabet, to paper, the printing presses, or the World Wide Web, our modernity is framed and phrased by the written word. Indeed, the great civilisations, such as ancient Egypt, Rome, and Greece, offer us a case study in the importance and power of writing. By most accounts, the history of writing also matches the history of schooling as we know it. In the eponymous grammar schools of England, we see a direct thread to the teaching of Greek and Latin rhetoric and

DOI: 10.4324/9781003179962-2

grammar. These epoch-making civilisations offer us the foundations of education and modern writing instruction.

Not only that, our creative breakthroughs and complaints about pupils' writing appear to have endured across the ages too. English language expert, Professor Richard Lloyd-Jones, noted that clay tablets recovered from ancient Sumeria (over 4000 years ago) exhibited teachers complaining about the deteriorating writing skills of their young pupils.[3]

It is a complaint as old as clay itself. *Pupils, eh?*

In this adventure, from clay tablet to a shining app-laden tablet, we are left with questions: *What have we learned about writing? What should we repeat and what should we reject as we seek to teach writing successfully?*

The roots of rhetoric and writing instruction

The origins of how we teach writing today truly began with the ancient Greeks. Writing had been taught and 'classrooms' developed in Sumeria, Egypt, and other great global civilisations, but it was the Greeks who developed the alphabet with vowels and consonants as we know it, making teaching, learning and, crucially, literacy, accessible to the masses in a way that is recognisable today.

In ancient Athens, writing would have played a visible and vital part of everyday life, from mundane notes, shopping lists, livestock, and crop records to sacred inscriptions on tombs and grand statues. The earliest written form worth remembering in Athens (around the eighth century BC) was the epitaph. These wise memorials on tombs were concise and incisive sentences, carved in capital letters for ease. In softening grief with the eloquence of a few words, we see writing emerge beyond simple everyday functionality, such as counting livestock, towards becoming an art form itself. The full expressive power of writing was beginning to be unleashed upon the world.

Once ancient Greece recognised the power of language and literacy, schools became more commonplace. Of course, when schools came along, questions about what curriculum should be taught followed soon after. Famed Greek thinkers, such as Aristotle, stepped in and established the keystones of rhetoric and writing instruction that still influence our approaches to writing today.

Aristotle would help coin the fundamentals of argumentation and story structures, as well as promoting the use of the popular discourse markers, such as 'so', 'therefore' and 'hence', to connect sentences and paragraphs into logical units of meaning. In essence, he would help serve up the substance that would give teachers the means to teach writing in an increasingly systematic fashion centuries later.

Fast forward to ancient Rome ...

What have the Romans ever done for us, you may ask? Well, apart from sanitation, medicine, education, wine, public order, irrigation, roads, a freshwater system, and public health, the Romans also raised the teaching of writing to new heights. In their systematic approach to writing, they encompassed writing instruction – from the functional to the fantastical – in a comprehensive manner that still guides our very modern notions of schooling, teaching, and the effective teaching of writing.

Enter perhaps the most important teacher in recorded history: Marcus Fabius Quintilianus – known more commonly as Quintilian. Born around 35AD, Quintilian would move from the Rioja region of northern Spain to study rhetoric in Rome, before himself becoming a treasured teacher. He would be celebrated by emperors and philosophers, along with countless pupils and their parents. Crucially, Quintilian distilled his teaching wisdom in the twelve books of the *Institutio Oratoria* (rediscovered in 1416, in an old tower in Switzerland). This crucial tome had the aim of offering a teaching sequence to 'educate the perfect orator'.[4]

In Roman times – and for many centuries after – writing was a means to serve eloquent and effective public speaking. The match between talk and writing – each mutually supporting one other – is recognised today, but in the Roman empire it was entirely central to the teaching and learning of writing. Quintilian himself summed it up: 'By writing we speak with greater accuracy and by speaking we write with greater ease [X. 7.29]'.

The curriculum for teaching writing described in the *Institutio Oratoria* was not developed in isolation. Quintilian stood on the shoulders of his great Greek forbears. For example, Quintilian drew upon Aristotle's influential rhetorical triangle for argument writing and talk (see Figure 2.1).

Logos – an appeal to reason, e.g. *If such writing guidance has endured for two thousand years, it must prove valuable.*

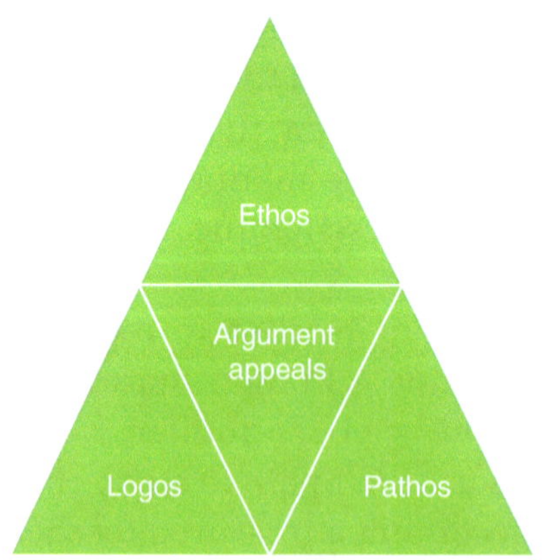

Figure 2.1 Aristotle's rhetorical triangle

Ethos – an appeal to the writer's own character, e.g. *I taught writing for nearly two decades, and I agree with Quintilian.*

Pathos – an appeal to emotions and beliefs, e.g. *Countless teachers, across four thousand years, have struggled with the same challenges when teaching writing.*

Quintilian described a comprehensive model for explicitly teaching writing, so that his pupils would develop the habits (known as 'facilitas') to make apt choices for any given writing task or speech. Our caricature of classical teaching being merely 'rote learning' is crushed by Quintilian. He was modern before his time, describing the learning of rules without models of writing as being like a ship drifting aimlessly without a steersman. He rejected slavish adherence to rules, instead encouraging 'guides' and not 'commandments'.

Imitation was held up by Quintilian as an essential ingredient for the effective teaching of writing. He developed the view that imitation was at the root of creative invention: 'For there can be no doubt that in art no small portion of our task lies in imitation, since, although invention came first and is all-important, it is expedient to imitate whatever has been invented with success.'[5] The concept of imitation was not derided, but instead celebrated as a path for the novice writer to walk along as they pursued the excellence of the expert. It offered manageable small steps, enabling a fresh and original voice to emerge over time.

Our modern notions of modelling writing were captured and crystallised by Quintilian. Reading and memorising models offered pupils 'an abundance of the best words, phrases, and figures'[6] for use in their writing. There would be lots of practice translating Greek writing to Latin, and Latin writing back to Greek, and transforming poetry into prose, or prose into poetry. Additionally, there would be an imitation of writing style from plain words to a grander, elaborate writing style, with reversals of that style too. There was word play, some direct imitation of good models, and lots and lots of effortful practice.

Given decades in the Roman classroom, Quintilian was not naïve to the writing issues of pupils, nor the struggles of teaching writing well. He viewed a 'corrupt style' of speaking and writing from his pupils, that 'revels in license of diction or wantons in childish epigram or swells with stilted bombast or riots in empty commonplace or adorns itself with blossoms of eloquence which will fall to earth if but lightly shaken...'[7] Clearly, Quintilian's twenty years of teaching meant he knew his pupils could be prone to a little pomposity. He described this as 'purple patches' – the origin relating to purple being the colour of emperors and so excessively decorated.

Two millennia later, the fundamentals of successful writing, and how to teach writing well, may not have changed significantly. As such, we can learn a good deal from the ancients as we seek out how to refine writing in classrooms today.

Writing with style (like the Romans)

Roman rhetorical devices describe the timeless patterns of language that have made speech and writing memorable for over two millennia, from deft repetitions, where words repeat and echo in our minds, to sentences displaying balance and force with a clever turn of phrase or a subtle shift of sentence structure.

What Quintilian and the relentlessly organised Romans brought to writing was a systematic approach that could be taught and replicated. The basics of grammar, handwriting and spelling (of a sort) were taught to younger pupils. Older pupils experienced a well-organised diet of rhetoric-fuelled writing. Today, it is the catalogue of rhetorical techniques that can still prove useful to teachers. We can recognise that Roman rhetoric – like the wisdom of Quintilian – offers useful resources for naming the tools of great writers. It can support our developing writers to hone their writing style and skills with increased precision.

It would be a mistake to prescribe here ancient rhetorical devices as some checklist for skilled writing. Instead, they have us describe ways to explicitly teach effective sentence building (more on this in Chapter 5). Though some of the terms appear grand and sophisticated, they simply offer labels for highly specific and expertly controlled sentence structures, repetitions, or carefully cultivated imagery. If we doubt their value and relevance, we should just look at their consistent use throughout the history of writing.

You can explore with pupils the power of repetition and rhythmic patterns with a selection of rhetorical devices that can be studied through instructive examples:

Rhetorical device	Definition	Examples
Anadiplosis (*'end/ beginning' repetition*)	A type of repetition in which the last word of one clause or sentence is repeated as the first word of the following clause or sentence.	'In the beginning God created the heaven and **the earth.** And **the earth** was without form, and void.' *The Book of Genesis* 'A precious boy who became **an artist**; **an artist** who became a legend.' *Describing Michelangelo in Art*

(*continued*)

Rhetorical device	Definition	Examples
Anaphora (*'Begin...begin... begin' repetition*)	A type of repetition which repeats a sequence of words or phrases at the beginnings of sentences or clauses.	'**In every** cry of every Man, **In every** infant's cry of fear...' *'London' by William Blake* 'To raise a happy, healthy, and hopeful child, **it takes** a family; **it takes** teachers; it takes clergy; **it takes** business people; **it takes** community leaders; **it takes** those who protect our health and safety. **It takes** all of us.' *Hillary Clinton*[8]
Epistrophe (*'...the end... end... the end' repetition*)	A type of repetition that repeats a sequence of words or phrases at the ends of sentences or clauses.	'...government of **the people,** by **the people**, for **the people**, shall not perish from the earth.' *Abraham Lincoln*[9] 'The time for the healing of wounds **has come**. The moment to bridge the chasm that divides us **has come**.' *Nelson Mandela*[10]
Asyndeton (*'short, blunt, no conjunction' sentences*)	A device which has a strong rhythmic pattern, but that omits conjunctions (such as 'and' or 'but').	'I came, I saw, I conquered.' *Julius Caesar* 'A bed, a stool, a table. Harsh, brief, poor lives.' *'The Werewolf', by Angela Carter*

Rhetorical device	Definition	Examples
Polysyndeton (*'and...and... and' sentences*)	A device that has a strong rhythmic pattern, which intentionally repeats conjunctions for added rhythmic effect.	'Let the white-folks have their money **and** power **and** segregation **and** sarcasm **and** big houses **and** schools **and** lawns like carpets, **and** books, **and** mostly – mostly – let them have their whiteness.' I Know Why the Caged Bird Sings, *by Maya Angelou* 'If there be cords, **or** knives, **or** poison, **or** fire, **or** suffocating streams, I'll not endure it.' Othello, *by William Shakespeare*

When pupils become sensitive to the rhythms explored in rhetoric, no advert or political speech is viewed, or heard, in the same way. Pupils better notice the subtle, unceasing rhythmic, rhetorical beat at the heart of writing, and they can, with explicit teaching, begin to imitate it, before going on to use it creatively and independently.

Along with rhetorical repetition comes the artful balancing act of sentence order. The following rhetorical devices stand out as useful for pupils who are beginning to craft their sentences with the aim of brilliant balance:

Rhetorical device	Definition	Examples
Tricolon (*The power of three sentences*)	A structural device that creates a series of three words, phrases or sentences that are parallel in structure, length, or rhythm.	'Joe is a healer. A uniter. A tested and steady hand.' *Kamala Harris*[11] 'But then, I am a teller of stories and therefore an optimist, **a believer in the** ethical bend of the human heart, **a believer in the** mind's disgust with fraud and its appetite for truth, **a believer in the** ferocity of beauty.' *Toni Morrison*[12]
Eutrepismus (*'First, second, third' sentences*)	A structural device that organises clauses or sentences numerically or in an ordered sequence for clarity.	'Firstly, the cells begin to divide. Secondly, the DNA replicates to form two copies of each chromosome. Thirdly...' *Mitosis cell division in science* 'First, when a white sauce is heated, the starch grains soften and swell. Second, the starch grains break open and release amylose...' *Gelatinisation in food and nutrition*

Rhetorical device	Definition	Examples
Antithesis (*'This versus that' sentences*)	A structural device that places two opposite ideas together in a sentence or sentences.	'It was the best of times, it was the worst of times...' A Tale of Two Cities, *by Charles Dickens* 'The Vikings are depicted as vicious warriors as well as sophisticated sailors and traders.' *The Vikings in KS2 history*
Chiasmus (*'This clause first, second clause that' sentences*)	A structural device for a sentence with two phrases or clauses, with the sentence part of the structure being reversed creating balance and symmetry.	'Ask not what your country can do for you; but what you can do for your country.' *John F. Kennedy* 'Despised, if ugly; if she's fair, betrayed.' *An Essay on Woman, by Mary Leapor*[13]
Anastrophe (*Yoda sentences*)	A structural device that changes the typical word order of a sentence for emphasis.	'Talent, Mr. Micawber has; capital, Mr. Micawber has not.' David Copperfield, *by Charles Dickens* 'One swallow does not a summer make, nor one fine day.' *Aristotle*

In many of these ancient rhetorical devices, we find names for the near-hidden rhythms and memorable structures of famous words and the skeletons of everyday sentences. Sam Leith aptly describes Roman rhetoric:

> Rhetoric is not a dry, narrow, out-of-date academic subject, but rather that is gathers in the folds of its robe

> everything that makes us human. Rhetoric is everywhere language is, and language is everywhere people are.
>
> *You talkin' to me? Rhetoric from Aristotle to Obama,* by S. Leith[14]

In a political speech, an advert, a poem, an exam essay or short-answer response, the relevance of rhetoric is writ large.

Writing in English and English schooling

In 1479, William Caxton brought the printing press to England. After years as a textile merchant in northern Europe, he was the first to produce a printed book in English (his own translation of 'The Recuyell of the Histories of Troye'). He would bring the press itself to Westminster, and in doing so change all our lives, transforming Quintilian's Latin into the written English language we know today.

Though the first books produced by Caxton were likely only for a small group of rich readers, the printing presses would soon make literacy, and writing, accessible to the masses. At this point, a printed copy of the Gutenberg Bible would set back an average clerk in England around three years' wage, and that was still considerably cheaper than those artful books handwritten by monks. In a short spell of time, technology advanced, printing proliferated, prices plummeted, and so writing became more commonplace for all.

The advent of the printing presses demanded some standardisation in spelling and punctuation. As headteacher Richard Mulcaster described in his book on teaching,

Elementarie, 'foreigners do wonder at us, both for the uncertainties in our writing, and the inconsistancie in our letters'. Spelling was simply a matter of personal taste before mass printing came along. Before the boom in printing, punctuation had few hard and fast rules. Indeed, the word 'punctuation' itself did not appear in the Oxford English Dictionary until 1539.

As the printing presses ushered in a modern age of common reading, books moved from being read aloud to being read silently and individually by many more people. This move meant that punctuation became prioritised to clarify meaning and to organise ideas. Punctuation was no longer simply about where a speaker should pause, though that limited conception would linger for centuries and influence the teaching of writing.

Radical punctuation developments were upon us quickly after Caxton's presses rolled across the nation. A Venetian printer, Aldus Manutius (1449–1515), is credited with standardising the full stop and the colon, and with printing the first ever semi-colon (he is also credited with inventing italics). Aldus also helped Caxton's multi-purpose slash to morph into the comma as we know it today – ushering in centuries of teachers struggling to teach their pupils how to use commas with accuracy.

Writing was becoming less a guide for speech-making and more an art unto itself. Many of the early attempts to communicate this shift in grammar did reflect how punctuation had been borrowed to describe pauses in speech. The comma, semi-colon, colon, and full stop had originally been arranged to describe the increasing strength and length of verbal pauses. Today, the guidance for pupils to pop in a comma when there is a brief pause can prove problematic, but the origins of this notion would have been accepted only a few hundred years earlier.

Writers the world over had to get to grips with punctuation and grammar, as the English language began its great standardisation, prompted by a few busy printers.

New standards of writing emerged, as reading and writing became more and more accessible and popular. The demand for schooling young people to write was wedded to more popular reading and writing. The sixteenth century was the age of the Renaissance in England (an intentional 'rebirth' of the Greek and Latin sensibility), so it was no surprise that the emerging education system borrowed heavily from ancient Rome and that the new 'grammar schools'[15] ushered in an education developed by Quintilian around sixteen centuries earlier.

In schools like St Paul's in London, created in 1509, the curriculum was in Latin and Greek, with the teaching of rhetoric and writing being central. Pupils would have experienced a daily diet based on the ideas of Quintilian, with lots of religious instruction too. Pupils would have experienced something of a bilingual education, with the continual act of translation from Latin to English and back again.

Great Renaissance thinkers like Erasmus (who helped found St Paul's and select their teachers) wanted to ensure that learning had the dynamism and principles of Quintilian's teaching of writing, but there was also a significant amount of narrow practice too, focused on the repetition of grammatical rules.

Young pupils in Britain, including an ambitious, novice writer called William Shakespeare, would have experienced a curriculum based on the Roman 'Trivium'. Comprised of grammar, logic and rhetoric, popular writing activities would have looked very familiar to an ancient

Greek or Roman pupil, for example, composing letters, verse writing, or devising orations. Writing and rhetoric were not found at the margins of the school curriculum; they *were* the school curriculum.

Given the teaching of writing was still wedded to speech, as the Romans intended, keen attention was given to the sounds of good writing. Grammar exercises would include playing with sentences so that they sounded good to the ear.

Shakespeare and his peers would have studied something like the Progymnasmata (taken, unsurprisingly, from Quintilian and ancient Rome). This fourteen-step system of writing exercises would have likely begun with taking a fable, such as Aesop's famous 'Hare and the Tortoise', as a model piece of writing. Pupils would have copied the story, contracted it, added to it, played with sentences from it, created wise sayings in response to it, compared it, argued about it, and, of course, performed it aloud.

The rich curriculum of imitation, variation, and numerous acts of creation was supplemented with a rigorous focus on grammar. Over time, writing and teaching textbooks did begin to be more prescriptive about the boundaries of accepted grammar, with the correction of 'false English' becoming a staple of the classroom. For every grammar school that was ensuring writing was a powerful mix of *ethos*, *logos* and *pathos*, there was one teaching slow, meth odical parsing of sentences (that is to say, the laborious analysis of each grammatical word class of every vocabulary item from a text in painstaking fashion).

Just as in the teaching of writing today, there were competing opinions about the failures of pupils' 'rustic' writing. These were expressed along with vehement arguments about how best to teach writing. What is clear is that the writing curriculum as we know it today has its origins in ancient Rome and has been slowly translated and updated.

Because the internet

The one constant of the English language is ceaseless change. Since the widespread emergence of schools in the sixteenth century, the teaching of writing has gradually evolved, but recent technology is rapidly changing writing.

We can look at this language change through the simple lens of sentence length. Back in the seventeenth century – arguably, the peak of punctuation use (they loved their commas and semi-colons) – the average sentence length was around 45 words. This fell steadily into the 30s during the nineteenth century, declining further into the 20s for us all today.[16] The simplification of sentences and writing styles was fuelled by a desire for accessible reading and 'white space' (that is to say, the areas on the page with no writing, which subtly aids readability). The ease of reading offered by 'white space' is particularly key when reading on screens. Today, it can be seen in the countless articles we read online that are structured with single sentence paragraphs.

A preference for shorter sentences – helpfully mimicking the rhythms of daily talk – has been accompanied by a modern-day punctuation minimalism. This hasn't all been driven by the impact of the internet. It is a long-standing shift. Back in 1906, H. W. Fowler's *The King's English* was recommending that the hyphen be dropped whenever 'reasonable' and that fewer commas were desirable.

Back in the 1940s, the American Rudolf Flesch began formulating 'reading ease' as a useable measure. Soon after, readability formulas became popularised, and so short seventeen-word sentences became sought after. By the turn of the century, welcoming white space and the simpler language of the World Wide Web was established. Writing in the classroom would slowly evolve too.

Along with the internet, technology has also ushered in useful word processing tools. Spelling and grammar checkers became common, then quickly became automated on our pupils' personal devices. Some early research found, perhaps unsurprisingly, that spelling and grammar accuracy was higher when pupils turned off the checking software.[17] Perhaps their active hard thinking could have atrophied in the knowledge that you can always 'Google it', or in the knowledge that the little wiggly red line can tell you the answer to a spelling or grammar mishap?

Language change is dynamic and live. Pupils need to know the difference between writing choices on WhatsApp and when undertaking an academic writing assessment in the classroom. Employing the casual prose of online chat – with its loosening of punctuation, dropping of spelling standards, sentence shortening, and similar – needs to be an informed choice.

There are some indicators that pupils' writing is generally becoming less formal, even when undertaking academic writing.[18] This unsurprising outcome isn't necessarily caused by the incursion of the internet into every corner of our day. A huge number of websites retain a faithful adoption of the norms of academic language and their habit of shortening proves sophisticated and stylish. The reality is that a more flexible, less formal approach to writing is centuries old and is likely a reaction against the strict standards of grammarians of the eighteenth and nineteenth centuries.

Technology developments are ensuring that writing is ceaselessly changing. There can be no denying that the internet has more written language than all the physical libraries in the world, with most pupils engaging with it in the electronic ether too. What of the future of handwriting, or spelling and grammar, as the internet age advances? How will the benefits of speech-to-text technology influence writing in the classroom? Will AI transform the teaching of writing in ways we can barely fathom? We are left making educated predictions. We can be confident that technology will adapt, and that writing will no doubt prove malleable too.

What will go unchanged will be the importance of writing. It will prove essential in all its varied forms, whether it is exercised by texting thumbs or in the hard work of handwriting, in our daily lives, in the world of work, and inside the classroom.

IN SHORT ...

- Writing, and the teaching of writing, developed systematically in the civilisations of ancient Greece and Rome. The roots of world-changing Roman rhetoric were the drivers for skilled and stylish writing.
- The first great teacher of writing – Quintilian – bears a uniquely modern sensibility. He recognised and helped revolutionise a systematic approach to teaching the writing process. Quintilian also recognised the value of imitation and modelling, alongside the dangers of 'purple patches' of prose.
- English grammar schools lived up to their name. Their curriculum was rooted in writing, with rhetorical exercises straight out of ancient Rome, alongside a developing focus on eliminating 'rustic writing' with a regimen of increasingly strict rules.

- Today, the internet, and instant access to technology, is changing writing. It was ever thus, but we should be circumspect about what is gained and what is lost when writing is mediated through technological tools.

Notes

1 Santayana, G. (1905). *The life of reason.* Cambridge: MIT Press.
2 Gaur, A. (1984). *A history of writing.* London: British Library.
3 Lloyd-Jones, R. (1976). Is writing worse nowadays? University of Iowa Spectator. April 1976. Quoted by Daniels, H. (1983). *Famous last words: The American language crisis revisited.* Carbondale, IL: Southern Illinois University Press. p. 33.
4 Murphy, J. L., & Wiese, C. (2015). *Quintilian on the teaching of speaking and writing: Translations from Book One, Two, and Ten of the* Institutio Oratoria *(Landmarks in Rhetoric and Public Address).* Carbondale: Southern Illinois University.
5 Quintilian, Eds. Murphy, J. J., & Wiese, C. (1987). *On the teaching of speaking and writing: Translations from Book One, Two and Ten of the* Institutio Oratoria *(Second Edition).* Carbondale: Southern Illinois University Press.
6 Ibid.
7 Quintilian (1985). *Institutio Oratoria, Book 12.* Harold Edgeworth Butler, Ed. Retrieved from: www.perseus.tufts.edu/hopper/text?doc=Quint.%20Inst.%2012.10&lang=original.
8 Clinton, H. (1996). Democratic National Convention speech. Retrieved from: www.americanrhetoric.com/speeches/hillaryclintontakesavillage.htm.
9 Lincoln, A. (1863). The Gettysburg Address. Retrieved from: www.abrahamlincolnonline.org/lincoln/speeches/gettysburg.htm.
10 Mandela, N. (1994). Inaugural speech. Retrieved from: www.essence.com/news/read-nelson-mandelas-groundbreaking-inaugural-speech/.

11 Harris, H. (2020). Vice President victory speech. Retrieved from: www.independent.co.uk/news/world/americas/us-election-2020/kamala-harris-speech-transcript-full-read-b1687603.html.
12 Morrison, T. (2004). Commencement Address to Wellesley College Class of 2004. Retrieved from: www.wellesley.edu/events/commencement/archives/2004commencement/commencementaddress.
13 Blain, V. et al. (1990). *The feminist companion to literature in English.* New Haven and London: Yale UP. Retrieved from: *https://en.wikipedia.org/wiki/Mary_Leapor#cite_note-Feminist-5*.
14 Leith, S. (2011). *You talkin' to me? Rhetoric from Aristotle to Obama.* London: Profile Books Ltd.
15 The notion of 'grammar schools' had a broader meaning in the sixteenth century – focusing more on the Roman curriculum than the very specific idea of modern-day grammar schools.
16 Moran, J. (2018). *First you write a sentence.* London: Penguin Books.
17 Galletta, D. F., Durcikova, A., Everard, A., & Jones, B. M. (2005). Does spell-checking software need a warning label? *Communications of the ACM, 48*, 82–86.
18 Constantinou, F., & Chambers, L. (2020). Non-standard English in UK students' writing over time, *Language and Education.* doi:10.1080/09500782.2019.1702996.

3 The not-so-simple science of writing

If you ever visit a nursery, make sure you seek out the story corner.

At Childhaven Community Nursery School in Scarborough, on the North Yorkshire coast, you can find one such story corner. In this particular narrative nook, you will find 'wonderful words' emblazoned on stars. Sitting on shining red cloth, there are small baskets labelled with 'problem', 'solution', 'setting' and 'character', containing objects to spark ideas for story-hungry children. Their big black 'Tales Toolkit' offers you the chance to read and relive the children's co-constructed stories. If you are lucky, you get to see the young children speak their sentences into life.

Seeing three- and four-year-olds making artful choices about their own tall tales can feel a little like magic. As they are compelled by seemingly effortless concentration,[1] you could be mistaken in believing the act of writing as natural as talk. The artful act of consciously selecting, shaping, reflecting, and revising writing choices[2] – exemplified so concretely in the corner of the nursery in Childhaven – reveals how young children can engage with the creative

DOI: 10.4324/9781003179962-3

act of writing with support and purposeful guidance through the writing process.

The details of writing development matter to how we teach. When the teacher takes on the act of handwriting and crafting sentences for the 'Tales Toolkit' in the story corner, it allows the children the extra time to think so that they can make deliberate story choices and talk their ideas into life. *Who is the hero of this story? Where is its setting and what can you find there?* Freed up from the potential trials of early handwriting skill, the children can construct stories with greater freedom.

The conscious crafting of writing – be it simple fables, or A level essays – becomes more technical and abstract as pupils move through school.[3] The act of story writing can retain its magical creative qualities, but the more complex the writing task becomes, the harder it is for pupils to manage their ideas and to communicate them fluently in their writing. When a pupil in year 5 is writing a balanced argument about protecting the local environment, they must consider an array of important knowledge and skills – handwriting and spelling; knowledge of sentence structures and the coherence of the text; the appropriateness of the content for the audience; the apt use of supporting evidence; ample knowledge of the local area and related challenges; meeting the goals for their argument, etc.

It is unsurprising that pupils find the act of writing so challenging *and* so rewarding when they succeed. It is unsurprising, given the sheer mental effort of holding all the necessary knowledge in their minds at any one time, that they fail to revise their writing much – limiting it mostly to minor word changes and some proofreading.[4]

We should consider writing as a creative art and as a science that we need to explore and better understand.

When you put the act of writing under the microscope, you can analyse how good writers pause to think and plan between sprints of rapid writing, whereas less effective writers pause more and get stuck on the mechanical aspects of writing.[5] All writers, even when seemingly effortlessly concentrated, write in a discontinuous fashion. They write six or seven words, then stop and evaluate their efforts before undertaking another writing sprint.[6] For novice writers, in those short moments they must draw on so much knowledge that writing can prove overwhelming. Their writing breaks down and they get stuck. And so, the expert work of the teacher proves essential at each stage of the writing process.

To help teachers to best manage the teaching of writing, and to carefully tend to pupils at each stage of the process, it is useful to explore a simpler model to steer this vital instruction. The Simple View of Writing (see Figure 3.1) is

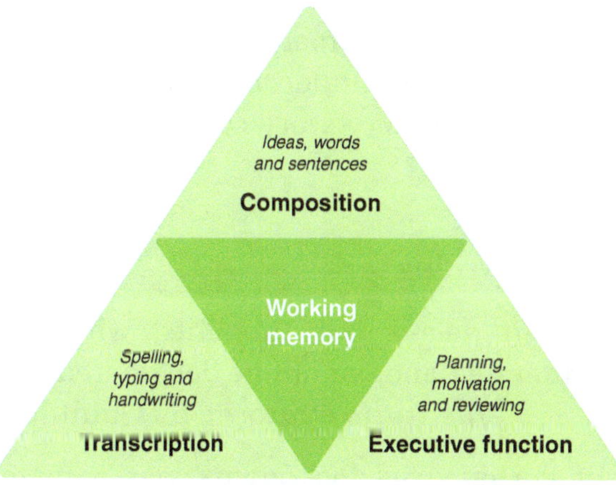

Figure 3.1 The Simple View of Writing

Source: Based on the model developed by Berninger et al.[7] and adapted from the model designed in the guidance report *Improving literacy in secondary schools.*

not so simple, but it is a helpful insight from the science of writing that can prove hugely valuable.

The researchers who devised the Simple View of Writing recognised what every teacher knows: strong and fluent foundations in spelling, handwriting, and typing – the basics of **transcription** – are a necessity for successful writing. They also characterised the act of written **composition** – which describes the brilliantly creative act of drawing upon a vast store of knowledge of written genres, sentence structures, vocabulary, and more, every time we compose a sentence. They also prioritised the vital work of our **executive function**. Put simply, this is our personal control centre that supports us to plan, sustain our attention, and stick to our goals when attempting the difficult task of writing.[8]

Breaking the act of writing down into these three identifiable elements can help both teachers and pupils. Though daily immersion in the act of writing will likely prove beneficial, it is the explicit teaching of transcription skills, composition, and the deliberate unpacking of the writing process that best helps pupils undertake that long and exciting journey from the nursery story corner to success in the GCSE exam hall.

Harping on about handwriting

> But a sluggish pen delays our thoughts, while an unformed and illiterate hand cannot be deciphered.
>
> *Institutio Oratoria*, by Quintilian

The experience of coronavirus lockdowns was a novel experience for pupils and teachers. As a parent, it was a strange pleasure to both see and support the home learning of both my children. My young boy, Noah – in year 4 during the first lockdown – was at a sensitive period in his writing. He was also struggling to sustain his attention on the act of writing (yes, dear reader, that is a euphemistic description). Crucially, his troubles with transcription were holding him back.

After a few months out of the classroom, Noah's typing skills had developed, with lots of daily practice on his computer, but his handwriting skill had noticeably degraded. At this point, it may be fair to ask the question: why harp on about handwriting? Won't Noah simply need to hone his typing skills for his technology-filled future?

The researchers who developed the Simple View of Writing show very clearly that handwriting remains a vital skill that is foundational to all writing development. Indeed, handwriting automaticity – being able to write fluently and legibly, with little conscious thought – can prove a unique predictor of the length and quality of sentence composition for young children.[9]

There is evidence that the physical forming of letters on the page, compared to typing keys, has advantages for developing writers and older pupils alike.[10] Indeed, even university graduates have been shown to struggle with a lack of handwriting fluency.[11] For Noah, his handwriting stamina had atrophied somewhat, meaning that his handwriting simply wasn't keeping up with his ideas. As a result, his composition was being compromised. Noah's attempts to communicate were being lost in translation[12] when he was expected to handwrite.

Writing can slow if children simply cannot generate the words and ideas to meet the task, but this act of composition needs to be supported by effortless handwriting and secure spelling.

Happily, in a relatively short time, Noah was able to boost his handwriting stamina. With fun, time-bound 'writing

Figure 3.2 Handwriting heights[13]

sprints' of five and then ten minutes, Noah was able to regain his fluency. It was important to balance the sometimes competing demands of handwriting speed and legibility. It quickly became clear that he needed some targeted feedback that his 'descenders' (letters with strokes below the baseline) – such as *p*, *q* and *j* – needed to discernibly drop below the baseline (see Figure 3.2). His 'ascenders' – in particular *b*, *d* and *h* – were inconsistent too.

Problematically, Noah thought more about maintaining a continuous cursive style than ensuring his writing was legible. As a result, close attention to an efficient mixed style, both cursive handwriting and print (letters formed separately), proved more helpful. A little attention on his letter formation made significant gains.

It can be easy to get bound up in debates about whether continuous cursive or print handwriting, or a hybrid of the two, is best for pupils' handwriting development. Though cursive proves popular, there is no substantive evidence it is better for handwriting development than print. Claims for the increased fluency and speed of the cursive style don't appear to be proven.

In the US, when 600 pupils across primary and secondary schools were compared, there was no difference in fluency or legibility.[14] In fact, the speediest writers (40 per cent of the pupils) used a combination of cursive and print styles. We should take care not to over-privilege speed and fluency at the expense of legibility and letter formation. A writing sprint may see legibility hampered to an unacceptable degree if not handled with care.[15]

Due to a combination of regular fluency practice and targeted feedback, Noah became more conscious and careful about his handwriting. Some metacognitive questions (that is to say, questions that helped Noah consciously reflect upon his own writing) helped him monitor and improve his handwriting, e.g.

- How would you rate your handwriting here?
- Circle your best word for me...
- Can any letters be improved?
- Are your letters the right size? Are your descenders the same length?
- Where is best to start writing this letter?
- What letter/s have you made most clear?

Of course, when evidence of a few weeks of handwriting is there before you in the pupil's book, you can keep a running record. Self-reflection and evaluation can be baked into the act of writing[16] – whether that is necessarily handwriting, spelling, word choices, or sentence construction.

Targeted interventions to improve the fluency of handwriting free up pupils' working memory to grapple with the complex chess game of writing.[17] This can also help remove the stigma that attends 'ugly handwriting', which can too often put pupils off writing altogether.[18]

Improving handwriting can be within the grasp of every pupil – young and old. Indeed, handwriting skill continues to develop well into the teenage years.[19] Offering young children a 'pen licence' will do little good if they do not receive specific instruction and feedback on what exactly they will need to improve (it may even turn pupils off writing). It is likely that notions of neatness will begin to frustrate pupils who struggle with basic letter formation. Given we know the most challenging letters to handwrite often prove to be the 'terrible ten' – *I, j, a, d, g, r, n, m, h,* and *z*[20] – we already have sensible starting points for instruction.[21]

We need to keep harping on about handwriting because a stark reality is that it matters in the classroom, the exam hall, and the wider world. Evidence shows teachers can rate pupils' writing negatively when their handwriting legibility is weak.[22] Perhaps even more importantly, weak handwriting can negatively affect a pupil's own judgement of their writing.[23] We want every pupil – young and old – to find the act of writing attractive, near-automatic, and always accessible.

Taking the time to tackle spelling

What is the difference between a sloppy spelling mistake and a more deep-rooted misconception about the spelling of a word? And does spelling ability *really* matter in the age of the spellchecker?

You *could* argue that spelling matters less given near-universal access to electronic spellcheckers. And yet, if you mistook 'duel' for 'dual', or 'casual' for 'causal' in a history essay, or 'infusion' instead of 'diffusion' in a science explanation, the spellchecker wouldn't detect an issue.

Though we should not overplay correct spelling as the be-all and end-all of writing, with targeted teaching and spelling support pupils can better self-regulate their own spelling when they write. When they are armed with a range of spelling strategies for unknown words, they can better fend off the narrow limits of their working memory. Put simply, it is worth taking the time to tackle spelling, especially given it can help improve pupils' writing quality (as well as improve their reading comprehension).[24]

The ability to spell accurately still holds a good deal of prestige in the classroom and in the wider world. Of course, you can be hugely successful, and even an influential writer, without being successful at spelling. Luminaries like Winston Churchill and Jane Austen were both known to struggle with spelling. But we should ask the tricky question: how many people who didn't make the history books were hampered by lots of spelling slips? In practical terms, how many people have missed out on their dream job because their application contained spelling errors? I would suggest many more struggling spellers were prevented from being recorded in the history books because their writing was compromised by struggles with transcription.

Pupils themselves quickly develop a keen sense of judging writing with spelling accuracy in mind. In research with Key Stage 2 pupils, where they judged narrative writing – with either 8 percent spelling errors, or no spelling errors – pupils deemed the stories with spelling errors to be poorly written and harder to read.[25]

Unhelpfully, this aversion to spelling errors can see pupils limiting the vocabulary choices they use in their own writing so that they do not make a mistake.[26] Ambitious vocabulary may be omitted and pupils' writing may suffer because of a lack confidence in their spelling ability. I have told many a pupil to be ambitious with their vocabulary regardless of spelling, but I observed them being inhibited all the same.

The natural urge to quickly finish a writing task with the minimum amount of mental effort can act against spelling accuracy. Accordingly, spelling often becomes a subtle measure of pupils' attitude and effort, with misspellings often being attributed to laziness and not necessarily a lack of understanding.

Pupils may have regular spelling tests, but often they can go untaught when it comes to commonly occurring spelling patterns. Expecting pupils to improve their spelling skills with regular testing – with seemingly unconnected lists of complex spellings – is unlikely to prepare them to use strategic spelling strategies when playing the more complex chess game of extended writing.

When pupils attempt to improve their spelling, they are learning more than just the 26 letters of the alphabet. They are aiming to match those letters to the 44 phonemes – or sounds – that are represented in around 250 different spelling patterns. It is therefore more efficient to focus on sounds in spelling, and then common spelling patterns, than to attempt to memorise disparate lists of words.

The act of noticing spelling patterns and recognising one's own spelling errors needs sensitive self-regulation. Happily, this can be taught explicitly. Quick, easy approaches – like young pupils putting on their 'check specs' when writing – can help young children be more attentive to the relatively minor edits for spelling. At Wyndham Primary Academy, in Derby, each classroom had an array of colourful spectacles for editing writing. Older pupils may not tolerate such props, but the principle is the thing. Ultimately, for all pupils, they can only check their spelling successfully if they have been taught common patterns and the relevant spelling strategies to do the job.

We are left asking: what are the most pertinent spelling problems and patterns to pay attention to for pupils?

The notion that English spelling is odd and dominated by erratic spelling exceptions is wrong. With solid foundations in systematic phonics teaching, pupils can make plausible spelling choices based on predictable patterns. Around half of all the words in English can be spelled with predictable sounds, with a further 36 percent being predictable except for one sound within the word.[27] Additionally, some of the language of phonics teaching – such as 'split-digraphs' (a two-letter vowel sound split with a consonant, e.g., 'a-t-e' in 'rated') – can be useful for teachers in naming spelling patterns.

Secondary school teachers, who teach subjects where spelling is assessed, too often go untaught in the benefits of phonics or spelling instruction. Uncertainty about how to support pupils abounds, and red pen corrections offer little help.

There are common spelling challenges pupils can master with timely teaching through all key stages:

- **Vowel clusters**. Most simple words in the English language have a clear consonant-vowel-consonant (CVC) structure. Individual vowel sounds can vary, such as a long /a/ sound being spelled with -a, -ai, -ay, -eigh, -ea or a-e. It starts to get even trickier when vowel clusters appear, and phonic patterns begin to vary, and the letter and sound correspondence is less obvious. Tricky vowel clusters include 'f**ee**t' and 'f**ea**ture', '**aeria**l' and '**ae**robics' (aer), 'milli**onai**re' and 'questi**onnai**re' (aire), and 'q**uee**n' and 'q**uee**r'.
- **Consonant doubling**. Most consonants offer a consistent, predictable single sound when compared to trickier vowels.[28] However, when pupils are faced with consonant doubles, they can struggle. It proves the highest category of errors committed by pupils in exams. For example, 'droped' is a common misspelling of 'dropped'. Typically, when the last three letters of a one-syllable word are 'CVC' then you double – such as

'big' to 'bigger' or 'sin' to 'sinner'. Spellings like 'muddy' and 'study' can be helpfully understood in this way. However, at other times doubling is not wholly consistent, so you can have 'melon' and 'mellow', or 'body' and 'shoddy'.[29]

- **Homophones**. A common issue is the presence of lots of commonly used homophones – words that sound the same but that have different spellings. There are around 500 homophones that feature frequently in school writing. Most homophones come in pairs, so the two possible spellings can be compared and practised, e.g. 'beach' and 'beech', 'new' and 'knew'. With explicit teaching, we can pronounce, pair, and practise these common spelling issues that often render spellcheckers powerless.
- **Morpheme patterns**. A vital progression for pupils' spelling ability is the recognition of morphemes – or, more simply, word parts – such as word roots, prefixes, and suffixes. This becomes essential when more complex academic terms are used in writing, e.g. photosynthesis (photo-syn-thesis). This implicit knowledge is used to learn new words and tricky spellings. You can target instruction, such as explicitly teaching a small number of prefixes (well over half of all prefixed words begin with 'un-', 're-', 'in-' and 'dis-').
- **Exception words**. Every pupil can have their own spelling idiosyncrasies. Some spellings are loaned from other languages or have rare combinations (words like 'coffee', which has a unique double letter spelling pattern). Many spellings of academic terms have clear Greek or Latin origins, so a little etymology unveils many spelling oddities (such as the silent b in 'debt' relating to the Latin roots of 'debitum').

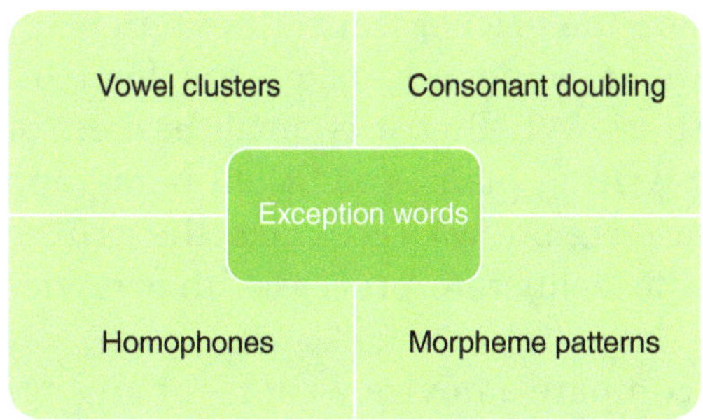

Figure 3.3 Common spelling challenges

Attention to spelling lists can be a starting point, but it will likely prove insufficient. With targeted teaching and structured practice, we can help pupils to better self-regulate their spelling when writing. For example, we can encourage the development of pupils' own personal spelling inventory (based on the common spelling challenges model in Figure 3.3) and align spelling practice with explicit vocabulary instruction.

Spelling doesn't prove so simple for many pupils, but teaching prominent spelling patterns, explicitly and consistently, will make a helpful difference.

Prioritise the writing process and planning for success

Let's return to the story corner in Childhaven.

Remember those little baskets labelled 'problem', 'solution', 'setting', and more? In these simple, active approaches to planning, we see the act of story writing simplified, scaffolded, and broken down into a manageable process. In such examples, we see each move in the chess game of extended writing made a little more explicit, a little more supported.

Shared writing, where the teacher transcribes and helps with the composition of sentences, takes the load off young, idea-laden writers. Whether it is small baskets or more elaborate essay-writing plans, pre-baked paragraph structures, or sentence stems, we recognise the crucial value of supporting the deliberate processes that novice pupils can follow.

It is useful then to compare a novice writer – of any age and key stage – with a pupil who is confidently on track to reach expert writer status:

Expert writer	Novice writer
Plans rapidly and often tacitly	Needs support, scaffolds, and nudges to plan their writing
Draws upon a vast store of background knowledge	Benefits from pre-writing activities that build background knowledge to support a given writing task
Possesses an awareness of audiences (even when that audience is a teacher or themselves) and their needs	Benefits from explicit attention to the needs and expectations of an audience for their writing
Possesses an awareness of genre, which is based on comprehensive wider reading. They know the 'rules' and when to bend and break them for effect	Benefits from explicit attention to the varied generic features of respective texts, along with practice of using these features in their writing

Expert writer	Novice writer
Possesses an awareness of revisiting and adapting their plan, along with revising and editing their writing	Benefits from explicit attention to updating their plans, along with revising and editing their writing
Possesses an awareness of evaluating their writing – with their reflections informing final revisions and edits before publishing	Benefits from explicit structures for self-evaluation and peer evaluation, along with deliberate teacher guidance and feedback

Take a moment to consider where your pupils may fit on the novice to expert continuum. It could be that for different tasks, or where pupils' background knowledge is uniquely strong, pupils may subtly slide along the continuum.

It can prove helpful to share the processes of real, expert writers with pupils. For example, the seminal American author Ernest Hemingway rewrote the final page of his great novel, *A Farewell to Arms*, at least thirty-nine times with the aim of 'getting the words right'. This offers an apt anecdote to make clear the importance of revising, along with the executive function to control, stay focused, and sustain the effort required to achieve writing success.

Whether you are seven or seventeen, the urge to write well can be helpfully supported, but even the most hard-working and expert pupils can struggle in the face of repeated failed attempts. Given the obvious degree of challenge, we should be wary of treating our pupils as would-be famed authors or mini historians, thereby bypassing the systematic supports required to advance from novice to expert writer status.

Real-world writers do routinely undertake a writing process – however idiosyncratic – with an audience, purpose, and goals in mind. Whether it is a journalist writing an article for a tabloid, an office worker crafting an essential email, a researcher writing a report about a new vaccine, or a children's book author coining their latest story, there will be familiar stages in the writing process that are undertaken by all.

The five-step model in Figure 3.4 offers a useable – and likely a familiar – cyclical writing process.

If we begin by considering how to support pupils to plan their writing, we quickly crash into the reality that many pupils struggle to plan their writing, or simply do not plan their writing at all. We should then consider: what are the pitfalls that commonly beset planning?

It can be frustrating for teachers who have explicitly taught planning strategies only to see them not translate

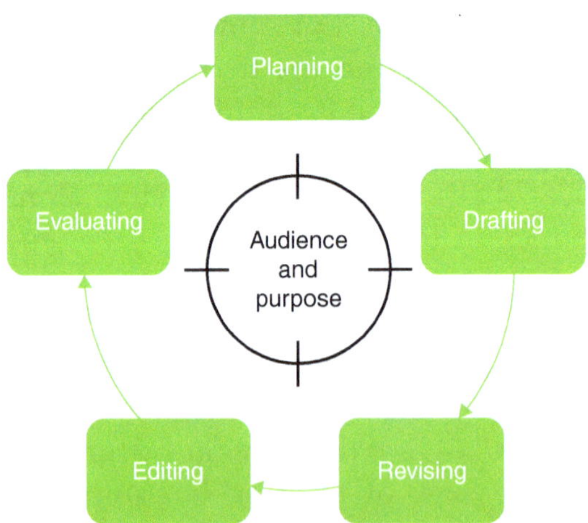

Figure 3.4 Five-step writing process

to pupils' independent writing. A common occurrence in exam-style timed writing is that the writing process becomes truncated, with the planning process being crammed into a few short minutes.[30] Pragmatic pupils quickly side-line the deliberative act of planning, especially when writing under the pressure of timed conditions.

Teachers with limited curriculum time can understandably focus in on exam-style writing processes. More expert young writers can quickly generate ideas from their deeper store of background knowledge, before organising these ideas into coherent structures. Unfortunately, struggling novice writers never quite internalise the writing processes, nor do they draw on background knowledge so easily. With too much focus on exam-style writing practice, more thorough planning instruction can be bypassed. Novice pupils get left behind their more expert peers.

Planning your writing – especially if the task is relatively short – can appear a frustrating and limiting act for many pupils. They just want to get going and write! The reality is that this positive urge can quickly run short of ideas. Unplanned responses often lose coherence, with pupils stuttering to an unstructured finish. The paradox we need to successfully communicate to pupils is that the time taken to plan should ultimately save time and energy. Indeed, greater creativity can be unleashed within a coherent structure.

Pupils often prove sceptical about the benefits of planning their writing. *'Will this get marked?'* is a popular refrain from savvy older pupils. And yet, research evidence indicates that writing quality and the amount of planning undertaken appear to be well matched.[31] Planning activities, such as written outlines, spider diagrams and rough full text, can offer small but positive effects on writing quality.[32]

There can be too much planning undertaken by pupils. I have observed very conscientious pupils who have written planning notes so extensive that it was tantamount to drafting the final product itself. Over-elaborate planning can be wasteful; and yet, most pupils err on the side of paltry attempts at planning.

The question of timing and how much planning is necessary is a matter for teacher judgement and not an exact science. In pragmatic terms, the more complex the task – and the more extended the writing – the more time is needed to deliberate and plan. If pupils are writing notes about an artist for their own remembering, very little planning is likely required; whereas, if a pupil is writing a full case study about the local area in geography in year 5, then more thorough planning is probably necessary.

When planning strategies become internalised and more automatic, the time needed to plan can be reduced, leaving greater scope for writing revisions, and more. The end goal of examination-style writing, for example, may see relatively speedy planning occur, but only because planning has been scaffolded and practised in much more depth, to the point of being near-automatic.

It is valuable to recognise that not *all* planning occurs before the act of drafting writing. We can describe the plans and knowledge gathering that occurs before drafting as 'pre-planning'. However, many a skilled writer returns to their plan at regular intervals to monitor their progress, revising it where necessary. We can describe this as 'reactive planning'.

If we return to the writing cycle, we recognise that even expert writing is messy and recursive, not pristine and linear (see Figure 3.5).

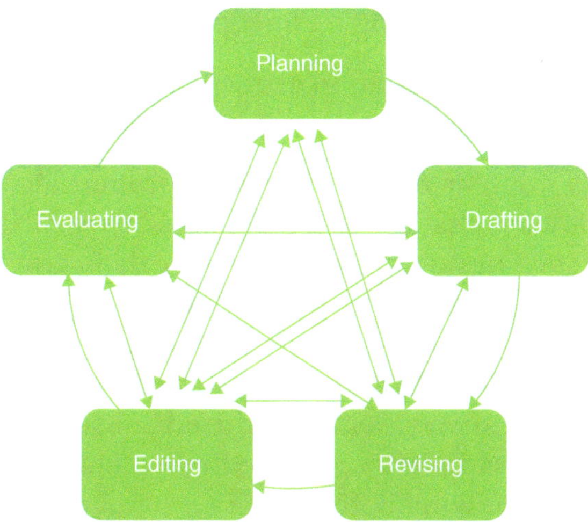

Figure 3.5 Five-step writing process (the messy reality)

A focus on making pupils acutely aware of audience can be a driver for effective planning. First, not *all* writing is audience orientated. If pupils are making notes about Expressionism in art, then the writing needs to be accurate and clear, but their notes are for them and therefore may not need to be elaborately planned. By contrast, 'audience-focused writing', such as writing a mystery story, or a history essay, requires audience awareness and sensitivity to their background knowledge and expectations.

Research indicates that thinking about audience when planning your writing improves writing quality,[33] with structured prompts and working with peers to consider the audience of their writing proving valuable too.[34] Sometimes a 'real' audience is artificial and time-consuming for teachers to plan for, but we can offer timely examples in every phase and subject domain. (For approaches to support pupils to plan their writing, see Chapter 7.)

Revising, editing, and developing a concept of quality

> It is easier to prune a tree than to grow one.
>
> Ancient Proverb

'I've finished!' is a popular refrain in the classroom. That race to the end of a task is all too common, but when it comes to writing, such haste to finish can prove damaging. It can compromise those vital later steps in the writing process: revising and editing.

It is important to establish what we mean by revising and editing, as they can be easily confused, misunderstood, and as such misapplied, or missed completely, by pupils. Let's use the following definitions:

- **Revising** is 'making changes to the content of the writing in light of feedback and self-evaluation'.
- **Editing** is 'making changes to ensure the text is accurate and coherent'.[35]

Too often, pupils have a narrow conception of revising their writing, so it becomes a thin version of editing, with a quick skim of spelling and grammar corrections, or the writing up of a 'neat' version.[36] Sound familiar? Another misconception is that revising your writing is simply 'adding more detail'. Back in the seventeenth century, the French thinker and writer Blaise Pascal claimed that one of his letters was longer than normal 'because I have not had time to make it shorter'.[37] That is to say, effective revision is often reshaping, reordering, and paring your writing down, not simply adding a flourish here and there.

What is clear is that the true act of revising your writing is laborious and it invariably makes pupils think hard, and so pupils avoid doing too much of it!

The situation that sees revision being relegated from the writing process is understandable. In many secondary school classes, writing activities can be constrained to a diet of note-making and single sentence answers.[38] As such, revision isn't commonly required or practised.

What appears to aid the act of revising your writing is to focus in once more on cultivating an awareness of audience during the writing process. In different research studies, activating peers as an audience can help motivate and focus pupils on crafting their writing with greater care. In one such example of audience-focused revising and editing,[39] the pupil acts as a peer editor, stopping at points where clarity is lost, and seeking clarification. This improved pupils' ability to identify comprehension problems in their own text. In addition, the 'author's chair' activity sees pupils read their work and receive critical feedback on their writing, so that they must explain their plans and any revisions to suit the audience and purpose of their writing.

Putting in the effort and successfully revising and editing your writing requires a concept of the audience for the writing and a clear concept of quality. Dr Royce Sadler put it best when he described how a pupil comes to:

> ...hold a concept of quality roughly similar to that held by the teacher, is able to monitor continuously the quality of what is being produced during the act of production itself and has a repertoire of alternative moves or strategies from which to draw at any given point.
>
> *Formative Assessment and the Design of Instructional Systems*, by Royce Sadler

Sadler describes, with near exactness, the writing processes of successful pupils. Of course, many pupils are not so successful in managing[40] their own writing process, and so they need support and ample deliberate practice.

Successful writing programmes, such as Self-Regulated Strategy Development (SRSD), help chunk down the writing process and explicitly model supporting writing strategies. For example, the SRSD approach models the strategy of using acronyms that prompt the revision of writing, such as DARE[41] to begin to help structure argument writing:

Develop your topic sentences.
Add supporting ideas.
Reject arguments from the other side.
End with a strong conclusion.

If pupils are not stopping to revise and edit at regular intervals, they can get to the end of the draft and feel overwhelmed by the scale of the job. Teachers can scaffold and chunk down this process by having 'editing anchor points', where pupils are encouraged to stop and step back from the act of writing to revise and edit. These anchor points can be structured by time (after 15–20 minutes of writing) or by selecting appropriate sections of a given writing task (for instance, after three paragraphs of an essay).

Studying model texts will likely help pupils develop a concept of quality that means that they better understand what revisions they might make. Of course, it can be very difficult to be your own best editor. Many professional journalists and authors rely on expert editors,[42] so we should not be surprised that pupils find it hard to edit their own writing efforts.

Once you have done with structural revisions, the arduous act of editing can begin.

Commonly, editing includes proofreading for grammar gaps, punctuation problems, and spelling slips. More modelling of editing practices and scaffolding of the writing process is necessary. For example, if the teacher, and pupil, each monitor an 'error record' from multiple pieces of writing (including any short notes in pupils' books where pupils didn't plan, draft, or revise comprehensively), then it can generate a personalised editing checklist – or style sheet – for pupils to use as a tool. Alternatively, some speedy error seeking on a writing model can offer pupils a fun, slightly more distanced, practice of editing. H. G. Wells is alleged to have said that 'No passion in the world, neither love nor hate, is equal to the passion to alter someone else's draft'![43] He was right.

We should not underestimate the mass of knowledge of grammar, sentence structure and spelling, that is needed to edit with confidence and skill. Invariably, it needs to be teacher-led, with the scale of the task shrunk to make it manageable for novice pupils. For example, editing with a focus on spelling and word choices can be undertaken, with pupils primed to seek out common spelling errors or encouraged to edit word choices more specifically.

Given the difficulties in revising and editing one's own writing, we can agree with famed author, Stephen King: 'To write is human, to edit is divine.'[44] These essential moves needn't prove mysterious divine powers. They should instead prove an integral part of daily classroom practice.

IN SHORT ...

- The act of writing may get increasingly complex as pupils move through school, but from the early years we can attend to supporting the writing process and breaking it down into small, manageable steps.
- The Simple View of Writing offers a clear tripartite structure from which to develop teachers' understanding of the science of writing.
- The development of both handwriting and spelling are vital transcription skills that are foundational for more developed and extended writing.
- Partially worked examples of writing, model texts, temporary scaffolds, anchor points where pupils stop to revise and edit, can all prove to be useful strategies to ensure that pupils overcome that desire to speedily shout, 'I've finished!'
- Explicit instruction in each part of the writing process – planning, drafting, revising, editing, and publishing – will be vital for pupils to go on to write independently with success.

Notes

1 Hughes, T. (1995). The Art of Poetry No. 71. *The Paris Review*, Issue 134, Spring 1995. Retrieved from: www.theparisreview.org/interviews/1669/the-art-of-poetry-no-71-ted-hughes.

2 Myhill, D. (2011). The ordeal of deliberate choice: Metalinguistic development in secondary writers. *Past, present, and future contributions of cognitive writing research to cognitive psychology*, 247–274.

3 Christie, F., & Derewianka, B. M. (2008). *School discourse: Learning to write across the years of schooling* (1st ed.). London: Continuum.
4 Graham, S., & Perin, D. (2007). A meta-analysis of writing instruction for adolescent students. *Journal of Educational Psychology, 99*(3), 445–476. doi:10.1037/0022-0663.99.3.445.
5 Alves, R. A., & Limpo, T. (2015). Progress in written language bursts, pauses, transcription, and written composition across schooling. *Scientific Studies of Reading, 19*(5), 374–391. doi:10.1080/10888438.2015.1059838.
6 Hayes, J. R. (2012). Modelling and remodelling writing. *Written Communication, 29*(3), 369–388. https://doi.org/10.1177/0741088312451260.
7 Berninger, V., Vaughan, K., Abbott, R., Begay, K., Coleman, K., Curtin, G., Hawkins, J., & Graham, S. (2002). Teaching Spelling and Composition Alone and Together: Implications for the Simple View of Writing. *Journal of Educational Psychology, 94*(2), pp. 291–304. Doi:10.1037/0022-0663.94.2.291.
8 Altemeier, L. E., Abbott, R. D., & Berninger, V. W. (2008). Executive functions for reading and writing in typical literacy development and dyslexia. *Journal of Clinical and Experimental Neuropsychology, 30*, 588–606.
9 Berninger, V. W., & Amtmann, D. (2003). Preventing written expression disabilities through early and continuing assessment and intervention for handwriting and/or spelling problems: Research into practice. *Handbook of Learning Disabilities*, 345–363.
10 Longcamp, M., & Zerbato-Poudou, M-T., & Velay, J-L. (2005). The influence of writing practice on letter recognition in preschool children: A comparison between handwriting and typing. *Acta Psychologica, 119*, 67–79. 10.1016/j.actpsy.2004.10.019.
11 Connelly, V., Dockrell, J., & Barnett, A. (2012). Children challenged by writing due to language and motor difficulties. In V. Berninger (Ed.) *Past, Present, and Future Contributions of Cognitive Writing Research to Cognitive Psychology*. 10.4324/9780203805312.
12 Graham, S., Harris, K. R., & Fink, B. (2000). Is handwriting causally related to learning to write? Treatment of

handwriting problems in beginning writers. *Journal of Educational Psychology, 92*(4), 620–633. https://doi.org/10.1037/0022-0663.92.4.620.

13 Wikipedia. Ascender (Typography). Retrieved from: https://en.wikipedia.org/wiki/Ascender_(typography).

14 Graham, S., Weintraub, N., & Berninger, V. (1998). The relationship between handwriting style and speed and legibility. *Journal of Educational Research 91*(5), 290–297. 10.1080/00220679809597556.

15 Graham, S., & Weintraub, N. (1996). A review of handwriting research: Progress and prospects from 1980 to 1994. *Educational Psychology Review, 8*(1), 7–87. https://doi.org/10.1007/BF01761831.

16 Graham, S., Harris, K. R., & Fink, B. (2000). Is handwriting causally related to learning to write: Treatment of handwriting problems in beginning writers. *Journal of Educational Psychology, 92*, 620–633.

17 Christensen, C. A. (2005). The role of orthographic-motor integration in the production of creative and well-structured written text for students in secondary school. *Educational Psychology, 22*, 441–453. doi:10.1080/01443410500042076.

18 Berninger, V. W., Mizokawa, D. T., & Bragg, A. (1991). Theory-based diagnosis and remediation of writing disabilities. *Journal of Educational Psychology, 29*, 57–59.

19 Santangelo, T., & Graham, S. (2016). A comprehensive meta-analysis of handwriting instruction. *Educational Psychology Review*. https://doi.org/10.1007/s10648-015-9335-1.

20 Prunty, M., & Barnett, A. L. (2020). Accuracy and consistency of letter formation in children with developmental coordination disorder. *Journal of Learning Disabilities, 53*(2), 120–130. https://doi.org/10.1177/0022219419892851.

21 The National Handwriting Association offers an excellent free downloadable booklet for teachers on helping handwriting. https://nha-handwriting.org.uk/shop/good-practice-for-handwriting/.

22 Graham, S., Harris, K. R., & Hebert, M. (2011). *Informing writing: The benefits of formative assessment*. Washington, DC: Alliance for Excellence in Education.

23 Meadows, M., & Billington, L. (2005). *A review of the literature on marking reliability*. Report for the National Assessment Agency by AQA Centre for Education Research and Policy.
24 Santangelo, T., & Graham, S. (2016). A comprehensive meta-analysis of handwriting instruction. *Educational Psychology Review*. https://doi.org/10.1007/s10648-015-9335-1.
25 Varnhagen, C. K. (2000). Shoot the messenger and disregard the message? Children's attitudes toward spelling. *Reading Psychology, 21*(2), 115–128. https://doi.org/10.1080/02702710050084446.
26 Sumner E., Connelly V., & Barnett A. L. The influence of spelling ability on handwriting production: Children with and without dyslexia. *Journal of Experimental Psychology. Learning, Memory, and Cognition, 40*(5), 1441–1447. doi:10.1037/a0035785.
27 Moats, L., & Tolman, C. (2009). Excerpted from *Language Essentials for Teachers of Reading and Spelling (LETRS): Spellography for Teachers: How English Spelling Works (Module 3)*. Boston: Sopris West.
28 Henry, M. K. (1988). Beyond phonics: Integrated decoding and spelling instruction based on word origin and structure. *Annals of Dyslexia, 38*, 258–275. https://doi.org/10.1007/BF02648260.
29 Bell, M. (2004). *Understanding English Spelling*. Eastbourne: Gardners Books.
30 Schuster, E. H. (2004). National and state writing tests: The writing process betrayed. *Phi Delta Kappan, 85*(5), 375–378.
31 Hayes, J. R., & Nash, J. G. (1996). On the nature of planning in writing. In C. M. Levy, & S. Ransdell (Eds.), *The science of writing: Theories, methods, individual differences, and applications* (pp. 29–55). Lawrence Erlbaum Associates, Inc.
32 Kellogg, R. T. (1993). Observations on the Psychology of Thinking and Writing. *Composition Studies, 21*(1), 3–41. www.jstor.org/stable/43501216.
33 Green, S., & Sutton, P. (2003). What do children think as they plan writing? *Literacy, 37*(1), 1–44.
34 Midgette, E., Haria, P., & MacArthur, C. (2007). The effects of content and audience awareness goals for revision on

the persuasive essays of fifth- and eighth-grade students. *Reading & Writing Quarterly, 21,* 131–151.
35 Education Endowment Foundation. (2021). *Improving literacy in key stage 2.* London: Education Endowment Foundation.
36 McCutchen, D., Francis, M., & Kerr, S. (1997). Revising for meaning: Effects of knowledge and strategy. *Journal of Educational Psychology, 89*(4), 667–676. https://doi.org/10.1037/0022-0663.89.4.667.
37 Pascal, B. (1658). *Les Provinciales,* or *The Mystery of Jesuitisme.* [Translated into English], second edition corrected, page 292, Letter 16: Postscript [Letter addressed to Reverend Fathers from Blaise Pascal]. Printed for Richard Royston, London.
38 Ray, A., Graham, S., Houston, J., & Harris, K. R. (2016). Teachers' use of writing to support students' learning in middle school: A national survey in the United States. *Reading and Writing: An International Journal, 29,* 1039–1068.
39 Graham, S., & Hebert, M. (2011). Writing to Read: A Meta-Analysis of the Impact of Writing and Writing Instruction on Reading. *Harvard Educational Review, 81,* 710–744. 10.17763/haer.81.4.t2k0m13756113566.
40 Education Endowment Foundation. (2018). *Metacognition and self-regulation guidance report.* London: Education Endowment Foundation.
41 Troia, G., & Graham, S. (2002). The effectiveness of a highly explicit, teacher-directed strategy instruction routine. *Journal of Learning Disabilities, 35,* 290–305. 10.1177/00222194020350040101.
42 Dear reader, I require a thorough and skilled copyeditor.
43 Quote Investigator (2016). 'No passion in the world is equal to the passion to alter someone else's draft.' Retrieved from: https://quoteinvestigator.com/2016/01/04/editing/.
44 King, S. (2012). *On Writing: A Memoir of the Craft.* New York: Simon & Schuster.

4 Grammar time

There are few topics in education – indeed, English life – that inspire fear, loathing and unfulfilled expectations quite like the subject of grammar.

Outside the classroom, the debates that attend the teaching and testing of grammar are as vehement now as they have ever been in modern education. Sadly, amidst these loud debates, too many teachers muddle along quietly and with little confidence about how to teach grammar to improve pupils' writing.

Many current teachers, myself included, are part of a generation where grammar went largely untaught. And so, when challenged about a conjunction we can crumble, or when we are asked about an adverbial we become anxious. My own 'grammar gap' began in school and extended to my teacher training (being trained to teach the English language no less). The harsh baptism of teaching A level English – with topics including basic grammar and how young children develop language and grammar – meant that I had to teach myself grammar.

Almost universally, teachers lack confidence in teaching grammar and explaining the effects of grammatical choices.[1] Even when teachers have a good knowledge of

DOI: 10.4324/9781003179962-4

grammar, they can lack confidence in teaching it.[2] It is a frustrating tale of innumerable missed opportunities.

It is easy to see how parents, otherwise highly confident with the content of their child's education, are puzzled by questions about fronted adverbials. When your eight-year-old asks, 'Dad, what is a determiner?', and you must furtively search Google for a plausible answer, it is understandable that you ask why this knowledge has passed you by.

It is also a fair challenge when highly distinguished writers ask questions about whether knowing technical terminology can translate to becoming a better writer. Clearly, you can become a famed writer without impeccable grammar knowledge (Wordsworth famously couldn't punctuate his own writing, so he asked a chemist, whom he had never even met, to punctuate some of his poems), though such a knowledge deficit is far from desirable.

Criticisms attending grammar teaching come from all angles. The more formal teaching of grammar has its roots in early grammar schools, centuries ago. At regular intervals since, grammar teaching has been routinely criticised as an ineffectual confining cage that produces 'square cucumbers'[3] and not skilled writers. Back in the 1960s, when grammar teaching plummeted out of fashion, it was challenged and described as having a 'harmful effect on the improvement of writing'[4] and simply being a waste of time.

After some decades in the wilderness, more formal grammar testing and teaching have seen a slow renaissance. The year 6 EGPS (English Grammar, Punctuation and Spelling) test – created in 2013 – has proven a prime subject for the rebirth of explicit grammar teaching, as well as attracting enmity. Esteemed critics, such as David Crystal,[5] have argued that question-types like 'circle the preposition' encourage a wasteful 'naming of parts', with pupils in danger of learning grammar labels without any meaningful application to their writing.

Fast forward a few years in the life of pupils and you move from the year 6 EGPS test to spelling, punctuation and grammar marks being issued in a plethora of GCSE exams. Too few secondary school teachers pay close attention to actively teaching grammar in their subject domain – largely because they don't know how. Consequently, much of what we deem grammar teaching proves to be little more than puffed up proofreading. A legion of grammar terms are assiduously taught and learnt in Key Stage 2, then just as speedily forgotten in secondary school and beyond.

The real problem with the teaching of grammar is not a single test with a few debateable terms, but instead the dearth of support offered to teachers, so that they can teach grammar effectively and consistently, across both primary and secondary schools. We should explicitly teach grammar knowledge, so that pupils can apply it to their writing, thereby enhancing both their accuracy *and* their creativity.

David Didau, in his book *Making Meaning in English*,[6] offers useful questions to steer pupils' grammar knowledge, so that they can better notice writing moves:

1. What options [grammar moves] are available?
2. Why was this one [grammar move] chosen?
3. What is the effect created?

You can apply these reading questions to a pupil writing a science report or a history essay. They foreground the need for pupils to understand and label grammar but, crucially, to understand it in use. If they understand the effect created by other writers, their instinct for imitation and adaptation can be cultivated so that their own writing practice is enhanced.

When teachers are supported to have a more confident understanding of grammar – with meaningful and well-targeted terminology – we can in turn help pupils to better notice, describe, and practise the moves of successful writers. For example, noticing how a writer uses adverbs for explanations in food and nutrition can lead to meaningful practice in writing fitting instructions for preparing food (should they stir 'quickly' or 'slowly'?). Additionally, in music, Italianate adverbs like *adagio* and *pianissimo* offer precise instructions on how to play an instrument.

Naming grammar and language choices clearly and precisely shouldn't be a worrisome addition; it should be baked into typical teaching, in food and nutrition and in every other lesson too!

It is crucial to have a shared language and to have an understanding of the basics of grammar as a common reference point. Let's start with the building blocks of grammar for great writing.

Word groups: the building blocks of grammar

If you were to attempt to address every aspect of grammar – its principles, patterns, and peculiarities – you would quickly fill a thousand pages. Instead, in the service of time-poor teachers, we should consider the essential building blocks of grammar that can support teachers to teach writing more effectively.

The keystones of grammatical knowledge, for pupils and teachers, are the words we choose to convey meaning. We can helpfully separate out the **content words**, which carry most meaning, from the **function words**, which cement sentences coherently together:

Content words	Function words
Nouns e.g. tree, dog, father	**Articles** e.g. a, an, the
Main verbs e.g. cut, bark, remember	**Pronouns** e.g. she, they, we
Adjectives e.g. green, angry, thoughtful	**Conjunctions** e.g. and, but, however
Adverbs e.g. nearby, quickly, generally	**Prepositions** e.g. after, on, under
	Modal verbs e.g. could, should, might
	Auxiliary verbs e.g. be, have, are

Nouns and adjectives

The most appropriate place to start is with **nouns**. Put simply, the academic language of school is 'nouny'. That is to say, school texts usually contain an array of dense **noun phrases,** like 'Industrial Revolution' in history, 'Avant-garde movement' in art, or 'computer-aided manufacture' in design technology.

We routinely encourage developing writers to extend upon descriptions of nouns to create *expanded noun phrases* (usually without labelling them as such). And so, 'a castle' becomes 'a towering Norman castle'. We encourage the sensitive selection of **adjectives** – words that describe nouns – like 'towering'. Too many adjectives and you get 'a towering, cold, wet, forbidding Norman castle'. Such an excess of adjectives can prove too much of a mouthful for any piece of writing in history.

Simply supporting pupils to notice that a great deal of academic writing, across the full curriculum, is characterised by complex noun phrases is a helpful start. We then grapple with the subtleties of subject-specific writing and nouns and adjectives. For example, in scientific writing you may typically strike out adjectives, especially given scientific noun phrases are already substantial. Conversely, in annotations in an art lesson, you would add adjectives to more accurately characterise nouns to capture apt artistic insights (think 'dynamic brushstrokes').

Verbs

Next, we come to **verbs** – the driving force of academic writing.

The old-fashioned description of a verb as a 'doing word' is problematic. Many verbs don't resemble doing. There are indeed **action verbs** – like 'kick', 'eat' or 'run' – but then there are very common **state verbs**. The four states that verbs generally fall into are:

- **Sense** e.g. see, smell, hear
- **Thought** e.g. believe, remember, know
- **Possession** e.g. have, belong, own
- **Emotion** e.g. love, want, need.

The most popular verbs are 'be' ('am', 'are', 'is', 'was', 'being' and 'been') and 'have' ('has', 'had' and 'having'), so there isn't a great deal of obvious 'doing'. As a result, pupils may mistake the noun 'boxing' for a verb in the sentence 'I hate boxing' because of this 'doing' fallacy.

We then run into the grammar reality that bedevils attempts to label words with accuracy. In the phrase 'doing word' we notice that 'doing' – normally a verb in English writing – becomes an adjective. A common misconception held by pupils is that vocabulary items can only be from a single word group. As the 'doing word' example shows, words can change their functions in sentences. This guides us to using lots of authentic examples in class to iron out singular anomalies and to better understand different verbs in use.

One of the signature features of school writing is the grammatical move of **nominalisation**. This describes when verbs are transformed into nouns. Read these two sentences and consider which one would be more apt for school science writing:

- We sweat through our skin so that we can cool our body down.
- The process of perspiration describes the excretion of fluid that evaporates from the epidermis to regulate body temperature.

It isn't hard to spot the 'school sentence'. Now, more specifically, nominalisation is the shift from 'sweat' to 'perspire', and then how the verb 'sweat' shifts to the noun 'perspiration'. It is one of the key reasons why academic writing is so nouny. It also characterises the simple notion of a lot of school writing using bigger words (with the suffixes '-ion', '-ance' and '-ness' being most common).

Now, we don't expect pupils to talk like a textbook, but as they progress through school we should encourage them to recast their language where appropriate in their writing. For instance, 'mix up' becomes 'vary', and then 'variation'.

Another type of verb that offers an ever-present feature of academic writing is the **modal verb**. When we write about places in the world, science experiments, or people in history, we are duly tentative because we are not certain in our claims, so we use modal verbs like 'could', 'might' and 'may'. For example, a historian who is writing about the causes of the Peasants' Revolt would naturally make cautious claims about how events 'may' have transpired.

Adverbs

Perhaps you want to add some detail and specificity to the verb in the sentence? This is when we typically introduce **adverbs** into our sentences. Adverbs tell us why, where, when, and how a verb is performed. Unlike nouns and verbs, adverbs can appear in all sorts of spots in each sentence. For example, we can have any of the following sentences:

- '*Hurriedly,* he wrote his book chapter.'
- 'He *hurriedly* wrote his book chapter.'
- 'He wrote his book chapter *hurriedly*.'

In the first example, we meet the much-maligned **fronted adverbial** ('*Hurriedly, he...*'). Is it purposeful to notice it in this example? We could plausibly describe how the fronted adverbial foregrounds, and subtly heightens, the sense of urgency and likely pressure to finish writing the book chapter.

Let's build a basic, but relatively successful sentence with an unconfident young writer like Ruby. She begins with a limited three-word sentence: 'The army assembled.' Let's help Ruby to build upon this 'kernel sentence' (a simple sentence with one verb):

- Ruby could add to and adapt the noun phrase to add greater specificity: 'The *infantry force* assembled.'
- Ruby could add an adjective for descriptive detail: 'The *shambolic* infantry force assembled.'

- Ruby could add an adverb to convey their exact movements: 'The shambolic infantry force *hurriedly* assembled.'

Ruby still has a relatively straightforward sentence, but one that is more specific and carries a great deal more information about the army force. With a few word groups added, with authorial intent, Ruby better conveys a state of disorder, and her sentence is more precise and interesting for it.

We shouldn't see pupils being taught word groups and their uses as a 'confining cage'. Instead, this is a handy tool for helping them to carefully craft their writing. As the 2014 National Curriculum states, explicit grammar knowledge can offer 'more conscious control and choice in our language'.[7] Let's open up more conscious choices for Ruby and her writing.

Making your point with punctuation

Once we have made a start on wrangling word groups into sentences, we recognise that we can better make our point with well-chosen punctuation. If words and phrases are the building blocks of grammar, then punctuation proves to be the cement.

In even the simplest of sentences, punctuation can prove vital. When faced with street signage like 'slow, moving traffic' or 'slow moving traffic', an appropriately placed comma could save a life.

We can helpfully divide the most important punctuation marks into two groups – **separators** and **terminators**:

Separators	Terminators
, Comma	. Full stop
; Semi-colon	! Exclamation mark
: Colon	? Question mark
() Brackets	
– Dash	

Other punctuation types

... Ellipsis

' Apostrophe

" " Quotation marks

- Hyphen

Well-chosen punctuation has the power to transform the meaning of words. As Theodor Adorno poetically put it: 'Punctuation marks are the stitches that hold the quilt of language together.'[8]

Let's take the simplest of greetings – 'hello' – and unpick how its meaning is altered with punctuation:

Hello!
Hello?
Hello...

We can instantly recognise the multitude of meanings and potential contexts for these sentences. The exclamation mark can help a sentence pulse with passion; the question mark converts 'hello' into a verb; the ellipsis offers us an air of mystery and endless potential. These are style choices that are not subject to hard and fast rules.

As G.V. Carey stated in *Mind the Stop*,[9] back in 1971, punctuation is conducted 'two thirds by rule and one third by personal taste'. Rather than a slavish adherence to notional rules, we should instead pursue common principles that lead to purposeful punctuation choices when pupils write. This doesn't mean lowering standards; it reflects an understanding of how writing has an array of creative moves.

Punctuation trends and patterns shift as our language changes over time.[10] The origins of punctuation were associated with speech and rhetoric, so separators and terminators originally referred to the length of pause for the speaker. As late as the nineteenth century, the semi-colon and the colon were used interchangeably. It is little surprise that pupils struggle to use semi-colons with uniform success, or face difficulties when offered limited advice like 'use a comma when you take a pause'.

Pupils using commas accurately and creatively in their writing can prove the stuff of celebration or calamity in the classroom. The comma is key for separating words, phrases, and **clauses** into manageable chunks for the reader. Put simply, there are two clause types:

- **Independent clause** contains a subject (a noun or pronoun) and a verb – so it contains all the components of a sentence in its own right, hence being <u>independent</u>, e.g. 'Jane needs to keep writing to succeed'.
- **Dependent or subordinate clause** contains a subject (a noun or pronoun) and a verb, but does not make sense as a sentence on its own – it is <u>dependent</u> upon another clause, e.g. 'if Jane wants to succeed in life'

Grammar time

We can go on to mark out the most common uses for commas:

Reason for comma usage	Worked example
To separate items in a list	I love pasta, pizza, lasagne, and ravioli.
To separate two independent clauses (along with a linking conjunction, e.g. but)	I love pasta and pizza, but I hate lasagne and ravioli.
To separate two clauses when you start the sentence with a dependent clause	Whenever I was starving, I ordered Italian food.
To separate out additional, but inessential, clauses that add information	The Italian restaurant, which closed every December, was thriving all summer long.
To separate out an **appositive phrase or clause,** i.e. additional, but inessential, information that further describes a noun	Queen Elizabeth I, the celebrated 'Virgin Queen', played a vital role in shaping the Tudor period.
To indicate a direct address	I think, Jane, you're wrong. *or* Jane, I think you are wrong.
To introduce direct quotations	Jane said, 'I loathe Italian food'.

Given that comma use is becoming less fashionable in modern, online writing,[11] we should not be surprised that pupils commonly underuse commas. Large-scale evidence from online writing has indicated that the Oxford comma (the final comma in a list, e.g. pupils need a pencil, pen, rubber, and scissors) has fallen out of fashion.

Using a comma to separate two independent clauses can be a matter of personal taste, rather than a glaring error. And so, we have a modern trend to drop commas that would add clarity to sentences. Let's expose these trends to our pupils – talking about their effects and effectiveness – so that they can make appropriate choices when they write.

The most common comma 'mistake' committed by pupils is likely the 'comma splice'. If we refer to our sentences with two independent clauses, and observe pupils omitting the conjunction, but adding in a comma, then we find our villain. For example, 'I love pasta and pizza, I hate lasagne and ravioli.' It is a common but often subtle misjudgement. It can be easily fixed by adding a conjunction, substituting the comma with a semi-colon (more on these later), or making each independent clause its own sentence. For example:

- I love pasta and pizza, **but** I hate lasagne and ravioli. [Add the conjunction.]
- I love pasta and pizza**;** I hate lasagne and ravioli. [Substitute in a semi-colon.]
- I love past and pizza**.** I hate lasagne and ravioli. [Create two separate sentences.]

The comma splice is commonly spotted in pupils' writing, and if deemed a problem can be quickly fixed with some concerted practice that explores accurate alternatives.

If this offers the notion of a clear 'rule', we need to remember that good writers will exercise their own good taste and break that rule when it is effective to do so. For example, 'I came, I saw, I conquered' – attributed to Julius Caesar – shows that the comma splice may work for rhetorical effect. When Stephen King noted, 'To write is human, to edit is divine', he was consciously deploying a comma splice. If novice writers are taught grammatical patterns consistently, then they themselves can begin to consciously break the 'rules' with stylish intent.

If we focus on punctuation that pushes the boundaries, we should spend a little time getting to know the daring **dash**. This flexible item of punctuation is beloved of poets and savvy pupils because you seldom get it 'wrong'. The dash, (not to be confused with its shorter cousin, the **hyphen**, which creates compound words like 'fast-moving') is brilliantly flexible. It can replace a comma, or a colon, and more, in a sentence. Its core function is to separate out a strong interruption in a sentence.

I am a fan of the dash and its strikingly visible way of separating clauses, and with a little instruction our pupils will be too. It is a pliable punctuation mark that could be deployed with confidence in writing across the school curriculum.[12]

It is apt to end an exploration of punctuation with the **colon** and the **semi-colon**. In recent times, a pupil's ability to deploy an accurate semi-colon or two in their writing has become a seeming indicator of their writing skill and a prerequisite for 'greater depth' writing in primary school. Often the last reminder in editing writing in Key Stage 2 can be to show off with a semi-colon. Though it *can* indicate a more advanced grasp of sentence structure and punctuation used for effect, it is easy to treat such punctuation usage as a tick-box exercise that does little to indicate the real quality of a piece of writing.

In the real world, beyond the narrow confines of pragmatic exam-writing criteria, the semi-colon is less popular.[13] The American writer Kurt Vonnegut argued that all the semi-colon does is 'show you've been to college'.[14] It can, however, come in useful for pupils' writing. The two main uses of the semi-colon are as follows:

- To separate a very detailed list where the use of repeated commas (or consecutive 'and's) may get confusing, e.g. 'The curriculum includes history and geography; art, design and technology; the sciences; and the core of English and maths.'

- To connect two independent clauses, thereby showing a relationship between them, e.g. 'She chose to study history and art; he selected geography and computer science.'

Once more, the application of the colon and the semi-colon needs to be considered as a point of accuracy *and* a matter of judicious choice. It is a writing move that can establish meaningful connections between sentences.

Colons most commonly introduce a list, an example, or a quotation, but they can also be used when contrasting two independent clauses in stark opposition. For example, in evaluating whether miracles prove the existence of God in a GCSE religious education argument, you may use the sentence, 'A theist sees miracles as proof of God: atheists view miracles as chance events.' Perhaps unsurprisingly, we could use a semi-colon in the exact same spot as the colon to similar effect. The colon subtly indicates a degree of balanced opposition that the semi-colon might not quite convey.

The more we scrutinise different writing tasks across the curriculum, the more we recognise that an accurate and creative repertoire of punctuation serves effective writing. In narrative or descriptive writing, it may be that an assortment of punctuation offers a varied rhythm for the reader that proves a success. For more analytical writing, you may use more colons to sequence logical lists, without adding in more dramatic punctuation moves like exclamation marks or ellipses.

When we teach pupils to make their point with punctuation, we ultimately teach them to make moves that both avoid obvious errors and exercise style choices that suit the task, and the subject, at hand. (Explore more meaningful punctuation moves in Chapter 5.)

When grammar goes wrong (and what to do about it)

Teachers should not shy away from the reality that there are many, often consistent, ways in which pupils' writing breaks down and loses sense.

Pupils themselves understand the value of accurate writing, even if they may be reluctant to pore over their own writing inaccuracies. Equally, they recognise that grammar errors can negatively influence the reader's perception of the writing.[15]

Various grammar experts have identified common errors[16] that hamper the clarity of writing. A sample of errors that are regularly found in pupils' writing includes these six (not-so-) deadly sins:

1. **Sentence fragments** (incomplete sentences) e.g. *Because the queen convinced him to murder.*
2. **Singular/plural possessive apostrophes** e.g. The Kings' subjects were angry.
3. **The comma splice** e.g. The experiment was unsuccessful, the temperature was not controlled adequately.
4. **Inconsistent verb tenses** e.g. The all-day battle was [past tense] a turning point, but William **dies** [present tense] weeks later.
5. **Double negatives** e.g. There aren't no crystals in the mixture.
6. **Lack of subject–verb agreement** e.g. I hope my parents buys me the present I want.

Understandably, many teachers may be thinking, 'I'd appreciate a steady diet of accurate capital letters for proper nouns and new sentences for a start!'

What are the teaching practices that best promote this rich language awareness[17] so that errors are eliminated and choices are exercised well?

Consistent research evidence indicates that teaching grammar, such as word groups and their functions, needs to be practically applied in the teaching of writing.[18] Debra Myhill and colleagues have developed the LEAD model[19] to exemplify good practice in grammar teaching:[20]

- **L**ink between grammar and writing
- **E**xplain grammar through examples
- **A**uthentic texts are explored
- **D**iscussion about grammar choices is undertaken

Let's exemplify the LEAD model with some authentic texts. We can explore the link between using an **appositive phrase** (an additional phrase or clause that describes a noun or pronoun) for additional information and effective writing, in geography or history, using authentic texts:

EXAMPLE 1:

> On 26 April 1986, reactor number 4 of the nearby Vladimir Ilyich Lenin Nuclear Power Plant, known to everyone today as 'Chernobyl', exploded.
>
> *A Life on Our Planet*, by David Attenborough

EXAMPLE 2:

> The Treaty of Versailles, arguably a significant cause of the Second World War, was signed on the 28th of June, 1919.

We can analyse the effects of the writers' choice of appositives in these two examples. The Attenborough example offers the essential 'aha moment' of revealing the infamous name of 'Chernobyl'. Not only that, but it also adds extra weight to the final word in the sentence, 'exploded' (read more about 'End focused sentence' in the next chapter).

In the history example, the appositive offers us the important additional insight into the historical significance of the treaty, not simply the factual recall of the date. The appositive is a versatile way of adding valuable information to any sentence. You can see how it can be applied to good effect in an array of academic sentences:

- Chernobyl, [appositive], is a stark warning of the dangers of nuclear power.
- Adolf Hitler, [appositive], was named German Chancellor in 1933.

A one-off lesson on adding in appositives isn't likely to stick. Instead, teachers will need to embed such grammar teaching into the substance of their curriculum and lesson planning, sustaining the LEAD approach over time.

The general grammar moves of academic writing

The grammar moves of academic writing are often intuitively known by teachers but not named and explicitly taught. And so, this writing knowledge can remain tacit and often fuzzy for our pupils.

An 'I'll know it when I see it' grasp of grammar and academic writing isn't likely to translate to teaching with clarity and confidence. If we can better define and break down the general grammar moves for academic writing, it can be taught more consistently.

The following 'top 10 grammar moves for academic writing' can form the basis of high-quality grammar teaching:

1. **Expanded noun phrases**. Academic writing is, in part, characterised by the sophisticated use of expanded noun phrases. In history, you might describe a

'fierce, intelligent queen', whereas in art you have 'two-dimensional practices' and 'twentieth-century abstract painters'. It is not always about adding words. Expanding noun phrases can lead to shorter, more accurate sentences. For example, 'it was very muggy and warm and then it rained really quickly' becomes 'high humidity followed by rapid precipitation'.

2. **Nominalisation**. Nominalisation is a characteristic move of academic writing, and it proves increasingly common as pupils progress through school. Active verbs become static information-packed nouns. For instance, we model the subtle language shift, so the verb 'change' becomes 'adapt' and then the noun 'adaptation'. And so potentially lengthy clauses like 'animals need to change to fit their environment' can be packaged up in the single noun 'adaptation'.
3. **Shrunken verb phrases**. We may expand noun phrases for precise academic labels, but we can shrink vague verb phrases for the same reason. For example, fuzzy two-word verb phrases can be reduced to a single verb: 'find out' becomes 'discover', 'hand out' changes to 'distribute', 'play down' changes to 'downplay', or 'take apart' becomes 'dismantle'. Equally, the use of strong verbs can eliminate the need for an extraneous adverb, so 'looked menacingly' becomes 'glared', or 'thought carefully' becomes 'deliberated'.
4. **Sophisticated synonyms**. Do you like your synonyms refined, cultured, urbane or polished? Every word a pupil selects for their academic writing is a choice that affects the style and formality of their writing. From Key Stage 1 onwards, the selection of synonyms is always occurring. It can be undertaken out of sight or in the heads of pupils, or it can be explicitly caught and taught, highlighted, and enhanced.

5. **Sentence signposts**. Cohesive and stylish extended writing contains a spine of conjunctions that act as 'sentence signposts'. They are so central to academic writing that we can too often take them for granted. If we are not careful, they can even appear invisible to the reader's eye, and so not applied with consistency by our pupils. 'First...furthermore...finally' can feature in arguments and explanations across the school curriculum.
6. **Tentative language**. Pupils mature as writers and begin to recognise that writing about history, religions, world geography, or literature is not about asserting certainty, but instead is defined by a tentative exploration. For example, modal verbs like 'may' and 'might', 'could' and 'should' best describe author's intentions, themes, and characters. Geographers exploring case studies of places in the world can speculate about what 'appears to'/'tends to' be occurring with people and the natural world.
7. **Additional appositives**. The use of an appositive phrase offers additional information about a noun or noun phrase. In many cases in school, like describing an artist in art, or analysing a character in English, this offers an opportunity for pupils to demonstrate their knowledge, e.g. 'Waterhouse's *Lady of Shalott*, the most iconic Pre-Raphaelite painting, portrays the...' An appositive can also add a varied sentence starter e.g. 'A landscape painting innovator, J. M. W. Turner depicted...'
8. **Additional points within parentheses**. Akin to appositives, popping additional information into parentheses – within brackets, dashes, or commas – is a skilled move used commonly in academic writing. Parentheses can be used by pupils to clarify their

explanations, e.g. 'The water cycle (also known as the hydrologic cycle) describes the movement of water from...'. They can also offer the option for an aside, e.g., 'Mary married Lord Darnley (also high in the line of succession) in July 1565, but they were soon estranged.'

9. **Right branching sentences**. A right branching sentence is the most common and clear sentence structure in academic writing. Put simply, it describes when the subject (noun) and the verb appear at the start of the sentence, for clarity, with additional details then branching off to the right of the sentence, for example, '**The Vikings used longships to travel** thousands of miles across the seas from their home in Scandinavia, combining wind propulsion and rowing power.'
10. **Use of the passive voice**. A common grammar feature in academic writing is the use of the passive voice. This describes when the subject of the sentence is the recipient of the verb's action. In science, if you are describing an experiment, you may convert the active voice ('We mixed the solution in the beaker') into the passive voice ('The solution was mixed in the beaker'). The focus in this instance is on the action being performed and the subject, so the pupil is removed from the sentence, thereby offering more scientific objectivity and a formal style.

Exercises in grammar moves to match an academic style can be active and well practised. When explaining the life cycle of plants in year 3, we may not use so many fancy terms, but instead simply model these academic writing moves. With older pupils, we can have the confidence to explicitly teach the moves, modelling their use before putting them into practice.

Pupils can observe some features in the academic writing they read, but they also need to write, revise, and edit their own grammar and style choices. They need ample practice in weighing up their effectiveness for the subject discipline, the task, and audience at hand. Success for struggling writers is likely to be slow and cumulative; however, with sustained planning, it can be achieved.

We aren't finished with grammar just yet...sentences are next up.

IN SHORT ...

- Grammar debates that attend the 'what' and 'how' of teaching grammar can cloud the development of best practice in the classroom.
- Many teachers lack the knowledge and confidence to teach grammar explicitly (beyond a few exercises) and to seize teachable moments with every act of classroom writing.
- Word groups offer the basic building blocks of grammar teaching, whereas punctuation proves the cement.
- Teachers need to be supported to recognise when grammar commonly goes wrong in pupils' writing, and to teach the common grammar moves that make up academic writing.
- Grammar teaching needs to be meaningfully embedded in writing, rather than constituting a series of separate exercises.

Notes

1 Myhill, D., Jones, S., & Watson, A. (2012). Grammar matters: How teachers' grammatical knowledge impacts on the teaching of writing. *Teaching and Teacher Education, 36*(2013), 77–91.
2 Cajkler, W., & Hislam, J. (2002). Trainee teachers' grammatical knowledge: the tension between public expectations and individual competence. *Language Awareness, 11*(3), 161–177.
3 Boechner, V. (2018). The square cucumber: Restoring student autonomy and confidence. *English Journal, 107*(3), 87–93.
4 Braddock, R. R., Lloyd-Jones, R., & Schoer, L. (1963). *Research on written composition.* National Council of Teachers of English.
5 Crystal, D. (2013). On a testing time. Retrieved from: http://david-crystal.blogspot.com/2013/05/on-testing-time.html.
6 Didau, D. (2021). *Making meaning in English: Exploring the role of knowledge in the English curriculum.* Oxon: Routledge.
7 Department for Education. (2013). English Appendix 2: Vocabulary, grammar and punctuation. Retrieved from: https://assets.publishing.service.gov.uk/government/uploads/system/uploads/attachment_data/file/335190/English_Appendix_2_-_Vocabulary_grammar_and_punctuation.pdf.
8 Adorno, T. W. (1990). Punctuation marks. *The Antioch Review, 48*(3), *Poetry Today* (Summer 1990).
9 Carey, G. V. (1971). *Mind the stop: A brief guide to punctuation.* London: Penguin.
10 The names of punctuation marks change over time too. Our modern day use of 'full stop' has competed with 'period' or 'full point'. Ben Jonson was fond of calling a full stop a 'prick'!
11 Crystal, D. (2015). *Making a point: The pernickety story of English punctuation.* London: Profile Books.
12 At this point, you may ecognize that I love dropping a pair of dashes into my sentences.
13 Crystal, D. (2015). *Making a point: The pernickety story of English punctuation.* London: Profile Books.
14 Vonnegut, K. (2005). *A Man without a country: A memoir of life in George W. Bush's America.* New York: Seven Stories Press.

15 Graham, S., Harris, K., & Hebert, M. A. (2011). Informing writing: The benefits of formative assessment. A Carnegie Corporation Time to Act report. Washington, DC: Alliance for Excellent Education.
16 Williams, J. T. (2014). The Phenomenology of Error. *College Composition and Communication, 32*(2), Language Studies and Composing (May, 1981), 152–168.
17 Denham, K., & Lobeck A. (Eds.) (2010). *Linguistics at School: Language Awareness in Primary and Secondary Education.* Cambridge: Cambridge University Press.
18 Myhill, D., Jones, S., & Watson, A. (2012). Grammar matters: How teachers' grammatical knowledge impacts on the teaching of writing. *Teaching and Teacher Education, 36*(2013), 77–91.
19 Chen, H., Myhill, D., & Lewis, H. (2020). *Developing writers across the primary and secondary years: Growing into writing.* Oxon: Routledge.
20 The brilliant team at Exeter University has freely shared useful presentations on the LEAD model here: https://socialsciences.exeter.ac.uk/education/research/centres/writing/grammar-teacher-resources/grammaraschoice/thegrammarforwritingpedagogy/.

5 Crafting great sentences

Where should we start with sentences?

Should we start with short sentences? Perhaps. They are a writing staple. Or maybe we should pay attention to long sentences, tracking their meandering attempts at meaning making, snaking their way through paragraphs, penned in by punctuation marks.

Then there are the sentences with the surprising clauses – dropping dramatically mid-sentence – that we may consider.

Just perhaps, we could begin with the controversial fronted adverbial, or we could just break the ru...

The number of meaningful moves when we write sentences is near infinite. It is a creative act so brilliantly complex that sentence writing has been described as a 'composition in miniature'.[1] Practising one sentence brilliantly may be worth more than writing out a hundred of them in haste.

It is crucial for pupils of all ages to control and craft a variety of sentences. Without such control, creativity can be stunted, and the pleasure and purpose of writing becomes limited. Undertaking the elaborate act of extended writing is a necessary end point – sentences do only make sense in

DOI: 10.4324/9781003179962-5

relation to one another – but we should not overlook the value of purposeful sentence-level practice along that path to writing in paragraphs and whole texts.

It is not a new teaching idea to improve pupils' writing by practising sentence composition. Erasmus, the Dutch philosopher and a godfather of early English schooling, wrote an influential book entitled *De Copia* in 1512, which can be roughly translated as 'the abundant style'. Borrowing ideas from our old friend Quintilian, Erasmus took individual sentences and explored their infinite variations.

For example, he took the sentence 'Your letter pleased me greatly' and then moulded and remoulded 147 different alternatives for it! Here are just some of his efforts:

- Your brief note refreshed my spirits in no small measure.
- From your affectionate letter I received unbelievable pleasure.
- Your pages engendered in me an unfamiliar delight.
- Your lines conveyed to me the greatest joy.
- The greatest joy was brought to me by your lines.[2]

Erasmus made explicit the vast array of potential moves for crafting sophisticated sentences. He was aware that novice pupils would imitate and create some over-elaborate 'purple patches' too, but this, he recognised, was a natural stage of development for pupils that could be explicitly addressed. The 'hundred ways to write a sentence' approach of Erasmus is useful, creative, and adaptable for all pupils of all ages.

Whether it is describing a violent Viking in year 3 or making precise and concise notes in GCSE chemistry, sentence crafting can shrink the complex act of writing down to a manageable move in the chess game. Sentence crafting is equivalent to practising scales and arpeggios in music. There is no claim that practising the scales alone will be sufficient for playing a concerto, but it does help to illuminate common musical patterns and it establishes the foundations to go on to move from novice to expert musician status.

When pupils revise and edit their sentences, it can too often be limited to checking for sloppy spelling, punctuation and grammar ('SPaG') or insubstantial advice to 'add some description'. With the explicit teaching of sentence variation – expanding them, combining them, and more – pupils can better notice the predictable patterns of effective writing.

Pupils do play the big game of extended writing in a range of subject disciplines in each school term, but if they do it too often they can be overwhelmed by the sheer mass of writing moves. Equally, with too many extended writing tasks, teachers are overburdened by excess marking, so precise feedback gets lost and struggling writers go on to repeat their mistakes, even hardwiring weaknesses into their writing habits.

The art of the sentence is about paying acute attention to brilliant variation (just like Erasmus). It is also about making timely and precise writing moves with sensitivity to audience, purpose, style, and substance.

Fragments to fantastic

It is time to return to a little more grammar, so that we can confidently get to grips with shaping sentences.

How can we best define a complete sentence? Many books on writing go to great lengths to wrangle an accurate definition. Too often, however, this results in little more than tricky terminology and pupil confusion. It can be addressed with greater accessibility.

Writing expert Stanley Fish helpfully described the basic components of a sentence as the 'doer – done – done to'.[3] That is to say, at the heart of a sentence is a subject (the 'doer'), a verb (the 'done') and, typically, an object (the 'done to') – though the last is not essential for a complete sentence. Take the simple sentence 'Alex cheered'. It has its subject (Alex) and its verb (cheered), so we are good to go. Now, 'Alex cheered' barely resembles the longer, complex sentence structures that pupils are routinely expected to write in the classroom, so we do need to build up the layers of structural complexity that are the basis for effective academic sentences.

First, we need to focus on a common flaw in pupils' sentence-level writing – the **sentence fragment**. As the term implies, a fragment is an incomplete sentence. A fragment typically omits a subject or a verb, omits both subject and verb, or it proves to be a stand-alone dependent clause, e.g. 'because of the impact of water pollution.' The sentence needs a subject, so a complete accurate alternative sentence would be '**The local ecosystem was damaged** because of the impact of water pollution.'

With explicit attention on sentence fragments, pupils can note the absence of a subject or a verb. Let's explore examples of sentence fragments:

- 'An era of punishment and progress' [Add in verb: 'It was'.]
- 'Everything south is the Southern Hemisphere' [Add in subject: 'of the Equator'.]
- 'Enters the stomata on the underside of the leaf' [Add in subject: 'Carbon dioxide'.]

When pupils are note-making, such as describing the process of photosynthesis, they can simplify their sentences and resort to writing fragments. We should be wary: if pupils are allowed to write repeatedly in sentence fragments, without explicit guidance, it could easily become a problematic habit. For example, if they are writing an argument about the afterlife in religious education, the tacit expectation is that pupils write in full sentences.

We can observe some deliberate rule-breaking going on with sentence fragments in the wider world of writing. It is popular in advertising to include sentence fragments when promoting a short, punchy slogan – for instance: 'See it. Say it. Sorted.' Equally, in narrative writing, a command does not require a subject and a verb in the same way (think 'Hello!' or 'Do not enter.'). These stylistic sentence fragments are rare in most school-based writing, so we can help pupils pay attention to this unique move as an exception.

When crafting fantastic sentences, pupils need to consider sentence complexity alongside completeness. A succinct two-word sentence such as 'smoking kills' can prove impactful. Adding the clarification 'smoking kills due to the effects of a range of damaging toxic chemicals' just doesn't have the same ring to it for the purpose of a punchy advert, but it may be judged a more effective sentence in scientific writing.

In primary school, pupils may move from writing short sentences in advertising language to extended argument writing in the same hour, and not note the subtle differences in writing style that are key to success. Explicit grammar teaching can help here to turn fragments into something a little more fantastic.

Developing more sophisticated sentences

We can study pupils' writing for answers about typical sentence composition and how to sustain sophisticated sentences.

Research featuring a sample of over 6000 written texts[4] shows that pupils increase their average sentence length with age, along with exhibiting a greater variety of sentence structures.[5] Mature writers move on from using lots of 'and's' to stringing together lengthier sentences, to using a more complex range of signposting vocabulary, such as 'however' and 'additionally'. More expert writers also exhibit longer noun phrases and more adverbial sentence starters (apologies to fronted adverbial adversaries!).

Is it any surprise that pupils' academic writing is defined by increasingly longer sentences? In Key Stage 3 geography, pupils are expected to write about 'less economically deprived countries' (LEDCs), with their 'economic indicators' and 'gross domestic product'. They simply must routinely use longer noun phrases to execute 'nouny' academic writing.

It is the creative and accurate control of complex sentences that marks out mature, expert writers.[6] In stark contrast, when struggling writers attempt longer sentences, they typically lose control of their expression and grammar.[7] Both novice and expert writers deploy short sentences in their writing, but older, higher attaining writers consciously deploy simpler, shorter sentences for rhythmic effect.[8]

To help struggling novices we can chunk down these complex sentences into their component parts. Let's break down a common range of complex sentences with a three-part structure: **front**, **middle**, and **end**. We can take a simple kernel sentence about the Battle of Hastings – 'The Battle of Hastings was fought in October of 1066' – and add to it to allow pupils to exhibit their understanding:

Front position	Middle position	End position
The Battle of Hastings was fought in October of 1066	, a seminal moment in the Norman Conquest,	resulting in the critical death of the English King, Harold Godwinson.
In the blood-soaked fields of East Sussex	, in October of 1066,	the iconic Battle of Hastings was won by the Norman army.
The Saxon and Norman armies fought for a nearly a full day in October 1066	(a brutal rarity in medieval wars)	in the blood-soaked fields of East Sussex.
In October of 1066	, the Saxon and Norman armies fought for nearly a full day,	in the blood-soaked fields of East Sussex.

Each additional clause displays both factual knowledge and historical interpretation about the battle and period. By tracking the main subject of the sentence – the Battle of Hastings – pupils can observe the patterns of the effective academic sentences that are typically hidden from the view of novice writers. Pupils can select their own moves for the **front**, **middle**, and **end** positions.

Two important sentence-level moves that feature in academic writing include **right branching sentences** and **end focused sentences**. A **right branching** sentence simple describes when the subject and the verb begin the sentence then all the additional information follows to the right. For instance, beginning with 'The Battle of Hastings was fought...' offers clarity and instant readability as there is no digging about for the crucial subject of the sentence. **End focused sentences** do the opposite job, placing the most crucial information at the end of the sentence. Key nouns are placed as the final words, or word, in the sentence, to attempt to gain a memorable emphasis.

You can observe end focus in David Attenborough's informational text, *A Life on Our Planet*:

> This book is a story of how we came to make this, our greatest mistake, and how, if we act now, we can yet put it right.

The end focus emphasises, with moral force, how we need to put 'right' the damage humans have wrought on the planet.

Over one hundred years earlier, another great advocate for our natural world, the iconic scientist Charles Darwin, ended his ground-breaking *On the Origin of Species* with an emphatic exemplar of end focus:

> There is grandeur in this view of life, with its several powers, having been originally breathed into a few forms or into one; and that, whilst this planet has gone cycling on according to the fixed law of gravity, from so simple a beginning endless forms most beautiful and most wonderful have been, and are being, evolved.

Note the power of 'evolved', sitting there at the end of the long, elaborate sentence with obvious end focus emphasis.

In the long, sometimes winding, sentences that describe scientific phenomena or interpret historical battles, the moves that decide what comes first and last in the sentence can prove decisive as to their impact. Paying close attention to sentence structure – including writing **right branching sentences** and deploying the **end focus** move – can pay off for our pupils.

Teaching sentence variation

Simple and punchy, or complex and contemplative, every sentence must serve its purpose.

For instance, in an argument, short sentences can offer a striking command, whereas lengthy complex sentences can offer essential detail, additional evidence, or contain clauses with necessary caveats.

Even the smallest sentence variations can have an impact. Let's begin with alternating punctuation **separators** to mark out an **embedded clause**:

- The class – loud as usual – arrived at the school library.
- The class, loud as usual, arrived at the school library.
- The class (loud as usual) arrived at the school library.

It may be subtle, but the use of the dash makes the loudness of the class appear the most essential information of the sentence. In contrast, the use of a pair of commas, doesn't draw as much attention. The brackets offer something of an aside (perhaps secretive or even embittered), offering more emphasis than the comma use but perhaps less than the pair of dashes. It is these minor writing moves, at a sentence level, that pupils can craft and draft, explore and edit.

Let's explore the four key variations available to pupils when writing sentences, illustrated in Figure 5.1.

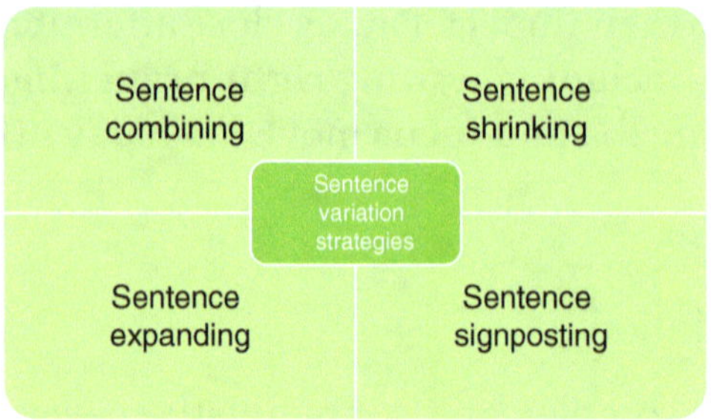

Figure 5.1 Sentence variation strategies

1. Sentence combining

The first line of defence against flimsy sentence fragments is a focus on sentence combining. It is an actionable step to move pupils from novice to expert writers, with particular benefits for novice writers.[9] At its simplest, it is the combination of two sentences into one complex sentence. For example, take the following two simple sentences:

- The boy was hungry. The boy ate pizza.

With sentence combining, it becomes...

- The hungry boy ate pizza.

Now, let's use a more sophisticated example from science:

- Biomes are areas of our planet with a similar climate and wildlife. Deserts and rainforests are biomes.

With sentence combining, it becomes...

- Biomes, such as deserts and rainforests, are areas of our planet with a similar climate and wildlife.

Pupils can combine these two sentences without losing clarity and be more efficient with their word use, given that the subject of the sentence – biomes – does not require repetition. Along with eliminating the repetition of the subject of the sentence, when two simple sentences have the same verb, it allows the writers to combine them into one efficient sentence. Take this example:

- I followed the algorithm. My partner followed the same algorithm.

With sentence combining, it becomes...

- My partner and I followed the same algorithm.

We can add to the complexity by bundling multiple simple sentences and combining them:

- The Earth's crust is the lightest rock layer. It is thin compared to other sections. It is around 5km to 70 km thick.

With sentence combining, it becomes...

- The Earth's crust is the lightest, thinnest rock layer, at around 5km to 70km thick.

The act of sentence combining can be made accessible for novice pupils, such as combining two sentences together with 'and' and other conjunctions. We should go on to test mature pupils with a paragraph with multiple shorter sentences, encouraging them to make decisions about appropriate sentence combining moves.

2. Sentence shrinking

Entire books have been written about the power and precision of shorter sentences. Verlyn Klinkenborg, in his popular book *Several Short Sentences about Writing*, appealed that you can 'say smart, interesting, complicated things using short sentences'.[10]

Bigger isn't always better.

Klinkenborg rightly recognises that writers, especially novice pupils, can trip over when they try elaborate sentence constructions. For those pupils whose sentences run on and on, invariably without control, shrinking sentences can prove an approach that strengthens their writing.

We shrink a sentence to gain power from precision. Let's take a flabby sentence:

- The rugged, weather-beaten adolescent boy gazed with hunger and adoration at the sumptuous banquet.

With sentence shrinking, it becomes...

- The rugged teen gazed hungrily at the banquet.

You may lose a little 'purple prose', but you gain in clarity.

Now, take the lengthy opening sentence of an online news article about climate change:

> Greenland's vast ice sheet is undergoing a surge in melting, with the amount of ice vanishing in a single day this week enough to cover the whole of Florida in two inches of water, researchers have found.[11]

With a relatively simple revision, this 37-word sentence becomes two more readable sentences of 12 and 20 words respectively:

> Researchers have found Greenland's vast ice sheet is undergoing a melting surge. The amount of ice vanishing in one day is enough to cover all of Florida in two inches of water.

The opening simple topic sentence on the melting ice sheet now offers a more accessible gateway into the text. We can get pupils to grapple with long Dickensian sentences, or similar, so that they practise shrinking sentences for the sake of clarity. A focused approach that practises a cleaner, more concise writing style can also help pupils avoid comma splice errors (one of the common comma errors described in Chapter 4).

An exaggerated form of sentence simplification is taking lengthy works and aiming for 'seven-word stories'. How about Frankenstein in seven words? 'Gifted doctor gives life but loses everything.' This compression of language – well-practised – offers pupils another writing move to exercise in an array of curriculum contexts, from short topic summaries to a succinct sentence with a persuasive punch, or abrupt rhythm changes in narrative writing.

3. Sentence expanding

Short, simple sentences can be impactful, but in a great deal of academic writing, pupils are encouraged to expand upon their ideas and the structure of their sentences. Akin to sentence combining, expanding sentences – adding clause upon clause – can convey more sophisticated and connected thinking.

Many writers about writing have appealed to simplicity and plain English.[12] Indeed, it is a useful challenge to ask: why write a sentence in 30 words when you could use 13? And yet, if Shakespeare had been edited and Macbeth had uttered 'Tomorrow' – and not 'Tomorrow, and tomorrow, and tomorrow' – how much poorer we would all be!

Sometimes sentences need expanding, to add analytical details and to make links, or to revel in rhythms and to convey sound and fury.

Sentence expanding can mimic the centuries-old stylings of Erasmus. If we take another of Erasmus's sentences from his *De Copia* – 'He is a total monster', we can play with word choices and sentence structure, as well as expanding upon the kernel sentence. For instance, we can expand upon the notion of his monstrousness by adding clause upon clause, adding physical and sensual descriptions:

- He is a total monster, **stomping through the school**.
- He is a total monster, **stomping through the school, screaming at petrified pupils**.
- He is a total monster, **stomping through the school, screaming at petrified pupils, shattering all semblance of tranquillity**.

With a character description in English, we can specify the sentence expansion by categorising each additional detail, e.g. What sights? What sounds? What smells? What emotions?

In history, you can introduce a significant historical figure with increasingly expansive information that displays historical understanding. Pupils can aim to translate basic notes and expand them into sophisticated sentences. Let's take the figure of William the Conqueror:

Who? William the Conqueror
Period? Medieval England
Significance? Led Norman Conquest, imposed the feudal system, and changed English culture.

Historical perspectives? Exercised power with brutal efficiency; reflected broader European change.

We can then combine this information into complex sentences (being aware not to overload any given sentence). Pupils need to make choices about what information to combine and expand in each sentence. For instance:

> William the Conqueror, the iconic English Medieval king, led the Norman Conquest that imposed the feudal system and fundamentally changed Britain, in an exercise in brutal efficiency. Significantly, William's conquest also represented wider European change, so we may helpfully reconsider the narrowing of this historical change as singularly 'Norman'.

Whether it is shrinking or expanding – or a combination of the two – modelling and making a talking point of these sentence-level moves can make for powerful writing practice.

4. Sentence signposting

Sentence signposting is as old as ancient Greece. Aristotle, in his early texts on rhetoric and grammar, made clear the value of connecting and clarifying the relationship within and between sentences.

Signposting sentences is now universally understood and is routinely simplified. It is common in today's classrooms to see acronyms for various conjunctions, such as FANBOYS (for, and, nor, but, or, yet, so), or WABBITS (when, after, because, before, if, though, since).

Additionally, the authors of *The Writing Revolution* have made the 'because...but...so' sentence scaffold famous.

It is useful to first categorise some of the high-value vocabulary we can deploy for sentence signposting:

Introduce / add on	Contrast / oppose	Cause and effect	Exemplify / support	Conclude
First	But	So that	For example	In conclusion
Second	However	Due to	For instance	To conclude
Furthermore	In contrast	Because	For this reason	In summary
Moreover	Conversely	Consequently	Particularly	Ultimately
In addition	On the contrary	Therefore	Significantly	Lastly
Equally	On the other hand	In the event of	In other words	Finally
Likewise	Nevertheless	As a result	Notably	In short

These sentence signposts can be handled clumsily by novice pupils if they are simply borrowed from a template or static word bank, without careful scaffolding and modelling.

Teachers can organise and deploy targeted signpost clusters with specificity by phase and the subject matter of the writing:

- **Year 5 balanced argument on school uniforms**. You can introduce your argument with the cluster, 'First... so that...as a result...', whereas the classic counter-argument can be framed by the 'In contrast...due to...however...' cluster.
- **Year 7 design technology new product brief**. You can begin with the cluster, 'First...furthermore...so that...' to introduce your product, followed by a cluster to focus in on one specific element of the product development, such as 'Due to...for this reason...notably...'
- **Year 10 biology summary of diffusion of cells**. You can begin with an introduction to diffusion of cells with the cause and effect cluster, 'First...so that...consequently...',

followed by exemplification of diffusion in the lungs with, 'For example...due to...as a result...'.

Carefully deployed – with exemplification, modelling, sentence stem supports, and more – these signposts can offer an understandable structure for our pupils to build successful sentences.

Choosing the right words to write

Pupils attempt to choose the right word for their writing hundreds of times every school day. Indeed, the broad and deep knowledge of words that pupils need to know so that they can use them for their own writing is a vital pre-requisite for successful writing and all learning.[13]

We simply cannot consider composing sentences without considering the choice of precise, appropriate, and ambitious vocabulary. Increasing sophistication of vocabulary across a range of writing genres is a pivotal development displayed by maturing writers.[14] The use of academic vocabulary becomes more common in all writing genres as pupils develop, but as pupils move through Key Stage 2 and on into secondary school academic vocabulary becomes a crucial factor in the daily act of writing.[15]

Pupils gain a greater sensitivity to word choices in their writing over time. This is made more likely through an inextricable combination of lots of reading of quality texts, along with a range of explicit teaching approaches that foreground language choices when writing. We are left asking: how do we best support this conscious awareness of words when pupils are composing sentences? How do we encourage revising and editing that helps pupils better calibrate their word choices?

Relying on the advice of professional writers to support pupils' language choices may prove problematic. For example, the famed aphorism (often attributed to Mark Twain) to 'find an adjective and kill it' flies in the face of useful teaching advice for our novice pupils. For a start, it wouldn't mesh with primary school writing assessments, nor sit well with GCSE examiners.

Some professional authors decry using adverbs or adjectives, but if you are annotating your artwork or writing a musical composition, such words are essential for the job. George Orwell prescribes that we should 'never use a long word where a short one will do',[16] but who decides what makes for a 'long' word, anyway? Exceptions abound in the classroom. Writing 'perspiration' instead of 'sweat' is essential if you are writing about the human body in science. In the classroom, the right word is often a long word.

There is no singular, sage advice that transforms pupils' vocabulary use when they are writing. Working new academic words into writing takes time. Vocabulary development is slow, intimately connected, and cumulative. Too often, we assume a tool like a dictionary or a thesaurus will do the job, but it proves an overly optimistic notion.

In her brilliant book *How Writing Works*, Roslyn Petelin describes 'thesaurus syndrome', where pupils stuff each sentence with long, overwrought vocabulary (remember the issue of 'purple patches' of prose first exposed by Quintilian?). Inappropriate attempts at using sophisticated synonyms, via a thesaurus or a dictionary, often appear comic. One pupil, seeing 'eat away' in a definition of 'eroding' in a dictionary, applied it to their own writing in unfortunate fashion, writing: 'Our family erodes a lot.'[17]

You can quickly find over one hundred synonyms for the word 'mistake'. Consider how much vocabulary knowledge a pupil needs to identify the right synonym for their writing. As a result, unconfident writers can tend to stick to the words they know and can spell.

Practically, we can select high-value vocabulary to teach, whilst also promoting 'word consciousness' so that pupils consider their choices carefully and reflect upon their effectiveness. 'Word consciousness' describes a broad curiosity about words, but it also captures that acute awareness of picking the right word at the right time.

A careful calibration of pupils' vocabulary choices can be cultivated through a range of teaching strategies:

- **'Simple <> Sophisticated'**. We can test Orwell's assertion about short or long word choices by continually comparing the impact of word choices, discussing and modelling alternatives that are simple or more sophisticated, for example, 'old' >< 'archaic', or 'ask' >< 'interrogate'.
- **Word triplets**. To scaffold vocabulary selection, we can supply pupils with a triplet of words to choose for their writing, thereby cultivating the crucial revision strategy of choosing the most apt vocabulary item. For example, in religious education, when offering a balanced argument about religious beliefs, a pupil could describe a given point with 'possibly', 'probably', or 'certainly'.
- **Thesaurus sprints**. Pupils need to have the use of the dictionary and thesaurus modelled and scaffolded. When revising narrative writing, you can get pupils to identify a small number of words to revise, before undertaking 'thesaurus sprints', with pupils rapidly selecting potential synonyms, before comparing and justifying their choices (just remember the dangers of 'thesaurus syndrome').

- **Word gradients**. One method to help pupils recognise the nuanced differences between synonyms is to select a pair of polar opposite words as anchor words, then generate five or six synonyms that provide a meaning gradient e.g. **happy** – 'content', 'joyful', 'delighted', 'down', 'dejected', 'despairing' – **sad**.
- **Singling out sentences**. When reading a text, from a textbook to a poem, pupils can be guided to single out the most successful sentence. By discussing and isolating the best vocabulary choices in these sentences, pupils enhance their awareness of words and create a store of useful vocabulary items for their writing.

It can be difficult for pupils to select words for their own writing without having been repeatedly exposed to these words in their reading. A rich, broad diet of reading will of course have a positive and cumulative effect on vocabulary knowledge, particularly when that word knowledge is activated during drafting, revising, and editing.

Pupils can be exposed to clichés in their reading too, so teachers can, over time, focus attention on what makes the difference between a predictable cliché and a more creative combination. For example, we can debate the relative merits of word pairings. Are 'finely balanced' and 'thinly veiled' predictable clichés? Are 'casual obsession' and 'pleasant misery' striking pairs?

Expert writers deploy metaphors and analogies to make their writing memorable. James Wood, in *How Fiction Works*, describes metaphors, similes and analogies as a 'little explosion of fiction'.[18] Exploring metaphors can enhance pupils' understanding. In science, debating whether the human genome is a blueprint or a recipe could provoke meaningful insights. In history, metaphors are baked into our language, such as the poetic 'Silk Road' – the ancient trade route that connected the Middle East and Asia with the Western world.

Let's ensure pupils can play the complex chess match of school writing by making successful moves with every sentence.

IN SHORT ...

- The act of extended writing is so complex, encompassing such a vast array of moves, that we should start with the manageable and meaningful acts of sentence composition.
- In simple terms, pupils need to be able to confidently craft multi-clause sentences to match the academic style of school writing.
- Pupils need to be able to manipulate a given sentence. Explicit practice in combining, shrinking, expanding, and signposting is the means to hone this ability.
- Pupils need to commonly make sophisticated vocabulary choices, but not suffer from 'thesaurus syndrome'.

Notes

1 Flower, L., & Hayes, J. R. (1981). A cognitive process theory of writing. *College Composition and Communication*, *32*(4), 365–387. https://doi.org/10.2307/356600.

2 Erasmus, D. (1978). Copia: Foundations of the abundant style (De duplici copia verborum ac rerum commentarii duo). Craig R. Thompson (Ed.), *Collected works of Erasmus*, Vol. 24. Toronto, ON: University of Toronto Press, 1978.

3 Fish, S. (2012). *How to write a sentence and how to read one.* New York: Harper Paperbacks.
4 Durrant, P., Brenchley, M., & Clarkson, R. (2020). Syntactic development across genres in children's writing: The case of adverbial clauses. *Journal of Writing Research, 12*(2), 419–452.
5 Ibid.
6 Applebee, A. N. (2000). Alternative models of writing development. In R. Indrisano, & J. R. Squire (Eds.), *Perspectives on writing: Research, theory, and practice* (pp. 90–110). International Reading Association. https://doi.org/10.1598/0872072681.4.
7 Myhill, D. (2008). Towards a linguistic model of sentence development in writing. *Language and Education, 22*(5), 271–288. doi:10.1080/09500780802152655.
8 Ibid.
9 Saddler, B., & Asaro-Saddler, K. (2010). Writing better sentences: Sentence combining instruction in the classroom. *Reading & Writing Quarterly, 29*(1), 20–43.
10 Klinkenborg, V. (2013). *Several short sentences about writing.* New York: Vintage Books.
11 Milman, O. (2021). Greenland: enough ice melted on single day to cover Florida in two inches of water. Friday 30 July 2021. *Guardian* online: Accessed online on 31 July 2021: www.theguardian.com/environment/2021/jul/30/greenland-ice-sheet-florida-water-climate-crisis.
12 Orwell, G. (1946). *Why I write.* London: Penguin.
13 Sullivan, A., Moulton, V., & Fitzsimons, E. (2017). *The intergenerational transmission of vocabulary.* Centre for Longitudinal Studies, Working Paper 2017/14.
14 Durrant, P., & Brenchley, M. (2019). Development of vocabulary sophistication across genres in English children's writing. *Reading and Writing 32*, 1927–1953. https://doi.org/10.1007/s11145-018-9932-8.
15 Deignan, A. (2020). The linguistic challenge of the transition from primary to secondary school. Podcast. Retrieved from: https://faculti.net/the-linguistic-challenges-of-the-transition-from-primary-to-secondary-school/.

16 Orwell, G. (1946). *Politics and the English Language*. Penguin Classics. London: Penguin.
17 Miller, G. A., & Gildea, P. M. (1987). How children learn words. *Scientific American, 257*(3), 94–99. https://doi.org/10.1038/scientificamerican0987-94.
18 Woods, J. (2009). *How fiction works*. New York: Picador.

6 Disciplinary writing

The game of school can be immensely enjoyable if you have the confidence to write skilfully. From the act of recording a science experiment to writing an explanation of the importance of the Amazon rainforest or crafting your own gothic tale, the school day is stuffed full of writing experiences.

And yet, many pupils struggle through this array of writing opportunities. Success is elusive. For too many it is more an 'unattainable, mysterious tacit code'.[1] The academic code of school writing is challenging because it is so multifaceted. Each subject discipline has its own chess match of genres and expectations, along with its own vocabulary and grammar patterns.[2]

We can detect close parallels in the writing tasks and genres pupils are given across different subject disciplines. In primary school, you may be taught 'writing to explain' in generic terms (e.g. 'use logical sequences and sentence signposts'), before putting that to work in scientific explanations. For instance, year 3 pupils would be expected to explain the life cycle of flowering plants. Fast forward to A level physical education examinations and older pupils are expected to analyse and explain how

 DOI: 10.4324/9781003179962-6

cryotherapy aids recovery from exercise. These tasks have an obvious connection, despite the difference in subject and phase, but there are also subtle and specific disciplinary differences in language between the two tasks that trip up many pupils.

We are left with a legion of questions about how best to help pupils develop as writers in the different subject disciplines in every phase and key stage.

It is essential to share specific examples of writing from the respective subject disciplines to begin to discern and describe the respective writing moves. For instance, a historical argument will have subtle differences compared to an argument in religious education or geography. The differences will go unnoticed by most pupils, and many teachers too.

Teachers themselves can gain a rich understanding of the specialness of writing in different disciplines by comparing different texts. Take a moment to read these two short extracts, considering their place in the school curriculum, as well as their nuanced differences in language and purpose:

1. The differences are caused by the Gulf Stream, a warm ocean current. Driven by westerly winds, the Gulf Stream begins in the Gulf of Mexico, flowing northeast where a branch of it heads towards Europe to become the North Atlantic Drift.

   GCSE Geography Edexcel B Student Book[3]

2. Fred looked out from behind the tree. The light of the moon filtered deep green to the forest floor, casting long-fingered shadows against the trees, and he could see only two bushes, both of them rustling. 'Who is it? Who's there?'...

   The Explorer, by K. Rundell[4]

The first text is from a geography textbook. The informational text encompasses a short, accessible explanation of physical geography. The noun phrases 'Gulf Stream', 'warm ocean current', and 'North Atlantic Drift' offer vital information to the reader, without the embellishment of adjectives and adverbs ('warm' and 'westerly' carry specific geographical meaning) that characterise fiction writing.

The second text is a fiction extract, from the brilliant adventure tale *The Explorer*, by Katherine Rundell. The varied sentence structures, along with the use of imagery and direct speech, reveal the rhythm and style of stories that are so familiar (and seemingly instinctive) to most readers and writers.

These two extracts helpfully exemplify some important parallels between fiction and informational text writing. For example, there are distinctive parallels in the sentence structures deployed. Each respective passage begins with a clear, relatively short, accessible sentence. They both follow this with a lengthy sentence with multiple clauses. They both use imagery ('branch' and 'long-fingered shadows'), but with very different effects. The textbook does so to convey the cause and effect of the Gulf Stream, each clause charting the movement of the Gulf Stream. Rundell, in subtle contrast, uses the multi-clause sentence to artfully describe the spooky sights and sounds of the Amazon being experienced by the character, creating a sense of building tension as we see it through Fred's eyes.

If we take the geography textbook example, we can consider how a geographer may be expected to write and communicate in subtly unique ways. The subject discipline of geography is an amalgamation of geology, economics, politics, biology, mathematics, and more. As such, it communicates that knowledge specifically, sometimes as a complex hybrid form of extended writing and cartography (mainly in the form of maps and diagrams). It would be a common classroom activity for pupils to write a short explanation of the Gulf Stream, complete with a diagram. The noun phrases, like 'North Atlantic Drift', may feature doubly, in both sentences and as a label on a diagram.

Pupils must also express their geography knowledge in words and sentences that display a sensitive understanding of academic writing in the subject discipline. For example, a GCSE pupil may be expected to routinely describe the impact of the North Atlantic Drift on the UK climate. A pupil stating that it 'warms the UK climate' is not wrong, per se, but we routinely expect more sophisticated, expanded sentences so that they can display their geographical understanding. 'Write in more detail' will likely prove inadequate feedback for the task of improving writing in geography. We can be more specific with some precise grammatical terms. For instance, we can ask pupils to use an expanded noun phrase to describe the Drift (e.g. 'warm Atlantic Ocean current'), along with encouraging the use of an adverb to more precisely characterise its degree of impactfulness (e.g. 'significantly' or 'marginally'), before asking for an additional clause to precisely describe *where* in the UK is impacted and *how* (e.g. 'with the western parts of the country experiencing milder winters as a result').

Compare the two right-branching sentences after three actionable writing moves:

1. The North Atlantic Drift warms the UK climate.
2. The North Atlantic Drift is a **warm Atlantic Ocean current** that **significantly moderates** the UK climate, **with the western parts of the UK experiencing milder winters as a result**.

Whether it is informational texts in geography, or adventurous fiction in English, understanding the ways of communicating in those domains makes their 'mysterious codes' more comprehensible. This is the stuff of 'disciplinary literacy'.

And so, what is 'disciplinary literacy' and how can it help teachers mediate all this complexity and better marshal approaches to teaching writing?

Disciplinary literacy has been described as 'an approach to improving literacy across the curriculum', with a crucial distinction that 'recognises that literacy skills are both general and subject specific, emphasising the value of supporting teachers of every subject to teach pupils how to read, write and communicate effectively'.[5] This definition is drawn from the Education Endowment Foundation (EEF) guidance report *Improving literacy in secondary schools* (which I had the pleasure of co-authoring with Robbie Coleman).

The central metaphor in the EEF guidance describes disciplinary literacy as a tree (see Figure 6.1). There is a depiction of the roots and trunk representing the general literacy knowledge and skills required by pupils, along with separate branches each representing the more specialist language and writing required of each subject discipline in the curriculum.

We can take the analogy of the disciplinary literacy tree further to usefully characterise how writing in a subject may change, and grow, as pupils move through school. If secondary school pupils must climb a mature tree with substantial branches, we can also recognise how with pupils in primary school we are instead considering a growing sapling, with slender, though still significant, branches of increasing subject specificity in the texts they are expected to read and write.

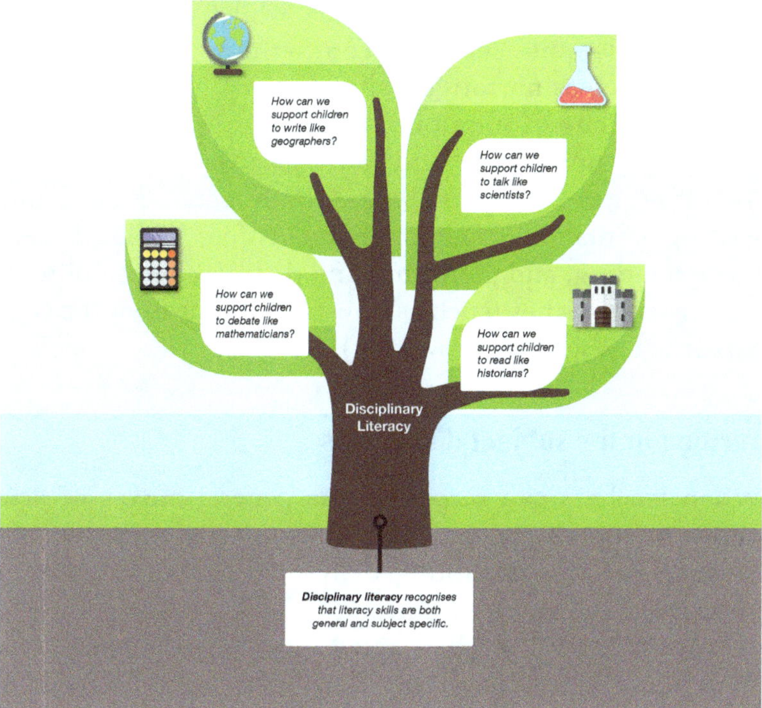

Figure 6.1 Disciplinary literacy

Source: Education Endowment Foundation (2019) *Improving literacy in secondary school guidance report*, London: Education Endowment Foundation.

In Key Stage 1, the writing tasks expected of pupils, such as recounting their personal experiences and story writing, do not typically put too high a demand on subject-specific knowledge and subject-specific language, allowing pupils to tackle transcription challenges, and more.

By Key Stage 2, pupils are having to grapple with increasing complexity and subject specificity. For example, when they are expected to write about why lemons can conduct electricity, they must deploy technical vocabulary, such as 'electron' and 'conductor', whilst using a formal writing style quite separate from writing genres familiar to them, such as narrative writing.

The challenge for pupils' writing grows quickly, and too many pupils falter and fall. The teaching of writing therefore needs to encompass both general academic writing demands (such as handwriting, spelling, sentence building, and planning) and distinctive disciplinary writing approaches (such as how to best represent the Gulf Stream in geographical writing).

Writing in the subject disciplines

When teachers can recognise the general moves of academic writing, it can help highlight subject-specific writing moves, whilst foregrounding distinctive differences within and across subject disciplines.

Primary school teachers must enact such subject style switching on a daily basis. Secondary school teachers, most typically teaching one subject discipline, can easily miss the changing, complex demands on their novice pupils as they write in different classrooms throughout the school day.

Let's explore disciplinary writing approaches by exploring a small sample of disciplinary writing practices.

Writing like a scientist

Learning science is hard. To be successful in science requires deep background knowledge, along with a confident grasp of how to apply the dense, abstract, and technical language of science in writing.

Let's explore some sentences in science. Michael Halliday, an influential British linguist, shared a range of sentence types, from typical everyday language to a more specialist, scientific sentence. We begin with an active, verb-laden sentence:

- Glass cracks more quickly the harder you press on it.

But with a few more moves, we can end up with:

- Glass crack growth rate is associated with applied stress magnitude.[6]

What differences stand out to you?

You may recognise some of the moves of academic writing in the final sentence: the expanded noun phrase, the right branching sentence, and the passive voice. The language is highly specialised, and far from the language of daily talk, or even the familiar patterns of storytelling.[7] We spy nominalisation again, as everyday verbs like 'cracks' and 'press' become complex noun phrases like 'glass crack growth rate' and 'applied stress magnitude'.

Is it any wonder that pupils increasingly struggle to both read the tricky academic code of science and apply it to their own writing?

In science writing, a pupil removes their personal presence from their writing (lopping off 'I' and other pronouns), so that it presents a more impersonal, objective stance. For instance, 'We analysed the data that revealed children consumed too much sugar' becomes 'The analysis of the data revealed children's excessive sugar intake'

In science, there is no goal to impress the reader with sparkling imagery or additional adjectives. Instead, precision is king and too much creativity with written expression is frowned upon. Indeed, in science GCSE, for example, if you select the wrong term, such as writing 'evaporated water' instead of 'vapour', you could lose marks in the examination.[8]

We should be wary of defining writing like a scientist through the narrow parameters of a science exam specification. The fact that pupils are not required to use full sentences or sentence signposts (bullet points are typically the preferred mode of exam answer for older pupils) may satisfy science examiners marking a pile of GCSE papers, but it can inhibit pupils' capability to think like a scientist in the classroom and beyond school too.

Using sentence signposts in science, like 'so that...due to...for this reason', can help pupils recognise 'cause and effect' relationships and important links between concepts. For example, in biology, we can recognise important relationships, e.g. 'People with type 1 diabetes can lower their blood glucose level by exercising ***due to*** increased respiration in the muscles.'

Classification is crucial to organise scientific knowledge, so words and phrases like 'comprises', 'included in', and 'an example of which'[9] all offer ways to categorise 'vertebrates' from 'invertebrates' in the animal kingdom, or distinguish between 'metals', 'non-metals', and 'metalloids' in the periodic table in chemistry. In science, the nouny writing needs to be coherently organised in writing, so structured note-taking – modelled by the teacher – is a must.

Seemingly minor writing moves in science can support pupils and better familiarise them with rare writing genres. For example, when pupils write up their scientific method for a given experiment, beginning a sentence with a strong verb – such as 'calculate', 'put', 'add', 'stir', or 'record' – helps pupils to be precise. Sentences have clarity when they begin with such strong verbs, e.g. '**Pour** 50cm^3 of hydrochloric acid into a flask' or '**Add** 50cm^3 of dilute hydrochloric acid to a conical flask using a measuring cylinder.'

Model sentence starters can be offered and compared as examples and non-examples as pupils practise the moves of method writing. These subtle moves characterise writing like a scientist, and they need to be foregrounded in reading and taught explicitly when writing up experiments and similar.

Writing like an artist (or designer)

Though we associate art and design with expression in paint and similar, or the production of creative products, there is a significant amount of writing required to succeed in the classroom. Writing in art and design has its own moves: pupils may typically kill off expressive adjectives or adverbs in scientific writing, but when it comes to art and design, these vocabulary additions are crucial.

Important artistic insights, observations, and independent judgements are all captured in the act of writing effective annotations on one's own art and design work. It is too often a writing genre that goes untaught. Pupils observe some successful examples, passing by impressive displays of model work, but the precise specificity of how to annotate effectively too often remains tacit to our novice pupils.

We can break down the micro-moves that define such annotation. In doing so, we can help pupils to avoid weak single-word annotations, or overlong descriptions, in favour of carefully crafted phrases:

- **Three-word summaries**. We can direct pupils to work within the parameters of three-word phrases, with verbs and expanded noun phrases likely to dominate, e.g. 'establishing initial ideas', 'exploring negative space', 'sombre monochrome colours'.

- **Artistic adjectives**. Describing art or design products demands descriptive language. Modelling and displaying an array of adjectives is a useful scaffold, e.g. 'complementary', 'decorative', 'delicate', and 'eclectic'.
- **Adverbs specifying action**. Annotation is often reflective and evaluative. Adverbs come in handy to express and evaluate one's artistic process, e.g. 'gently', 'dynamically', 'vigorously', and 'rapidly'.
- **'So that' sentences**. A valuable signpost in art and design is the 'so that' phrase. It is handy to scaffold the 'so that' sentence to guide the language of self-evaluation, e.g. 'because...so that...on the whole'; 'first...so that...as a result'; 'Initially...so that...consequently'.
- **Evaluative phrases**. Pupils, understandably, enjoy the creative act of making, but self-evaluation proves difficult. Short, simple scaffolds to aid their thinking can make this tricky process more manageable, e.g. 'I concluded...', 'The product successfully...', 'In retrospect...', and 'Upon further reflection...'. Design briefs and written reflection tasks are predictable and often acceptably formulaic, so scaffolds can be introduced, varied for effect, and then carefully faded out.

Pupils in art and design are routinely expected to critique their own work and the work of others. A key expectation is that pupils utilise the specialist vocabulary that describes the formal features of art, e.g. line, form, tone, colour, pattern, and composition.

It is common for novice pupils to describe their visual language but fail to explore the 'how' and 'why' of their artwork or design choices. Once more, sentence signposts for 'cause and effect' are useful starting points to scaffold pupils' writing, and these can be combined with evaluative conclusions, e.g.

- 'I used... [formal feature] ... so that...which ultimately...'.
- 'I utilised... [formal feature] ... due to...which resulted in...'.
- 'This piece contains... [formal feature]... because... with the overall effect of...'.

A useful genre to practise writing and to consolidate knowledge of artists, their works, and methods is the gallery label. These are the short paragraphs that adorn the walls of galleries to concisely explain works of art. They offer a meaningful and manageable writing task to get pupils to build their knowledge and use specialist language. A simple scaffold can structure the gallery label paragraph:

1. Artist and artwork (year): XXXXX, XXXXX (year)
2. Biographical details: XXXXX
3. Art movement and influences: XXXXX
4. Formal features: XXXXX

Read this example gallery label paragraph and reflect upon the writing moves deployed:

> Edvard Munch, the prolific Norwegian painter, is most famous for his iconic expression of angst, *The Scream*. His innovative Expressionist paintings explored illness, emotion, and mortality. The fiery bright colouration, bold brush strokes and curved lines convey a chaotic emotional state. The curved, screaming figure blends into the background, like the scream is tearing through nature.
>
> *The Scream*, by Edward Munch (1893)

You can observe artistic adjectives, such as 'prolific', 'innovative' and 'chaotic', along with an appositive ('the prolific Norwegian painter'). Then there is the use of a tricolon ('illness, emotion, and mortality') along with a simile ('like the scream is tearing through nature') for a subtle explosion of style.

By focusing on a short piece of writing – within parameters of 50 to 70 words, or a limited number of sentences – you can encourage pupils to exemplify and practise using specialist vocabulary, along with selected writing moves in art. Crucially, it will help pupils both understand and remember the artwork they are researching, as well as improve their writing skill.

Writing like a historian

Writing in history demands a difficult combination of broad historical knowledge, understanding of concepts that span across historical periods, rich vocabulary knowledge, and familiarity with a range of complex writing genres. In short, history writing is hard!

Contrary to caricatures of history as a mere timeline of kings and queens, history is a rich tapestry of narratives with competing claims that are 'slippery and elusive'[10] for many of our novice pupils.

You can broadly describe a movement from writing records of history in primary school with a more personal and accessible 'story-led' approach to a later focus on increasingly sophisticated and abstract argumentation in secondary school.[11] Pupils can go from narrative writing describing Samuel Pepys burying parmesan during the Great Fire of London in primary school to writing a sophisticated extended essay in secondary school about how religion may have held back medical advancement in the 1600s, without an awareness of the changing notions of writing like a historian.

If exploring the Gunpowder Plot in year 2, a common approach would be to write a wanted poster or a newspaper article (with scaffolding) explaining the events of the plot. Pupils are transported to the event, before exploring it chronologically and personally, with a heavy reliance upon a familiar narrative style when they write.

In Key Stage 3, they would be more likely to explore more abstract arguments that grapple with competing accounts and interpretations of the Gunpowder Plot. Exploring the causes and implications of the events, making ethical judgements, and giving weight to historical viewpoints would all be expected, along with the common moves of academic writing. Such writing is more separate from their lives and more abstract and, put simply, it is harder to write.

As pupils read and develop an understanding of writing like a historian, simple signposts like 'because' and 'so' are left behind for more subtle, mature alternatives. Historians do not write with the uncritical stance of 'X causes Y because...'. Instead, they try to better characterise the cause – is it a root cause, a catalyst, a trigger, a pre-condition, or an underlying cause?[12] Pupils can use language to express causal links that display a more nuanced understanding than 'because'. Phrases like 'X was a necessary prelude to Y', or 'X offered the platform for Y' display a more nuanced stance of a historian exploring complex concepts like 'significance' and 'change'.

Starting with simple sentence signposts is helpful, especially for primary age pupils, but as pupils progress in the subject discipline, being saturated in good quality historical writing and having a broader range of writing moves is also necessary for them to develop as writers of historical accounts and arguments.[13] With a focus on quality reading, teachers can build a bridge from narrative genres to historical arguments, from the primary history curriculum to its secondary equivalent.

In texts like John Hatcher's *The Black Death: The intimate story of a village in crisis 1345–1350*, a semi-fictional retelling of history offers pupils an accessible entry point,[14] exposing them to chronological personal stories that bring the period to life. The action of such narratives may be action-packed, but even academic essays can be active and full of clashing historical claims and strong verbs, e.g.

- Verbs for claims: 'suggest', 'assert', 'believe', 'emphasise', 'intimate', and 'advance'.
- Verbs for agreement: 'endorse', 'support', 'attest', 'acknowledge', 'corroborate'.
- Verbs that challenge claims: 'discount', 'refute', 'reject', 'deny', and 'repudiate'.

To write in history is always richer than word lists and five-paragraph essay outlines. It is irreducible to an easy formula. But we can characterise it as an intriguing hybrid of story and argument (along with note-making too), with pupils moving between these different writing approaches with confidence. To do so, pupils need explicit teaching to practise the moves for each writing type and to explore their boundaries and overlapping features.

Writing like a geographer

Let's return to writing like a geographer.

First, consider a major city in the world that you know well. Is it relatively local or international? Is it developing, emerging, or advanced?

Now, evaluate some of the challenges faced by this city. Is it deindustrialised? Does it have sustainable natural resources? What about its environment? Does it have significant geopolitical relationships and issues?

The challenge to evaluate a complex, changing place in the world in a few short paragraphs is a common task for a geographer. Writing a case study – or 'assessing' or 'evaluating' the development of a place – contains a lot of writing moves. A pupil is expected to refer to evidence consistently and offer a balanced argument that makes tentative judgements, as well make lots of logical connections that display a deep geographical knowledge.

Notions of a 'balanced argument' in geography are often abstract and hard to grasp for novice pupils. When year 8 pupils are expected to argue about palm oil, they need enough knowledge to write in a balanced fashion. Quite naturally, they get wrapped up in 'my side' of the argument, often lacking the background knowledge, along with the structural shifts, to convey depth and 'balance'. Argument scaffolds and familiar sentence signposts are a necessary, but insufficient, support for pupils wrestling to communicate tricky, multifaceted concepts, such as 'interdependence' or 'sustainable development'.

When pupils are dealing with the multiple moves of geographical writing, they can habitually make underdeveloped, simplistic assertions. This can arise from a combination of a lack of background knowledge of place and gaps in their knowledge of how a geographer writes.

How geographers communicate about a place in the world with a balance of factual accuracy and tentative language, about potential change and the causes of that change, is complex. We return to that problematic 'mysterious code' that trips up so many of our young writers.

Let's take a recognisable topic of natural disasters and earthquakes. Pupils evaluating the impact of an earthquake can write sentences like 'Earthquakes cause lots of damage in the areas they hit'.[15] If pupils' exposure to earthquakes is bound to films and television, then it is understandable that they may remember these dramatic film representations over the more common, but minor, earthquakes that do little damage and simply don't make the news.

Geography teacher Mike Simmons has devised an accessible 'double development' approach to challenge misconceptions and to develop writing so that pupils revise initial sentences. A few questions challenging the assertion of the strength of some UK earthquakes can lead to a better redrafted sentence with appropriate tentative language: 'Earthquakes measuring more than 6 on the Richter scale **have the potential** to cause severe damage **if** they hit centres of population. For example, a magnitude 7.0 earthquake struck Haiti in January 2010.'[16]

We can observe how specific evidence, with geographical vocabulary and background knowledge, combines with the common moves of academic writing, such as tentative language, expanded noun phrases, and sentence signposts.

We can attempt to summarise and compare some of the parallel writing moves across a range of subject disciplines:

Science	Art and design	History	Geography
Dense noun phrases e.g. 'applied stress magnitude'	Dense noun phrases e.g. 'Abstract Expressionism'	Dense noun phrases e.g. 'Emancipation Proclamation'	Dense noun phrases e.g. 'tensional plate margin'
Passive sentence structures to convey objectivity	Adjectives to convey precise visual language	Tentative language and model verbs e.g. 'may' and 'could'	Appositive phrases to concisely describe geographical phenomena
Sentence signposts to convey logical sequences in describing scientific methods e.g. 'Firstly...as a result...In conclusion'	'So that...' sentences to convey self-evaluation of technique	Sentence signposts to claim causes and effects e.g. 'Due to...' and 'A direct consequence...'	Sentence signposts to describe places clearly e.g. 'Firstly...For example... In the event of...'
Bullet point lists to convey scientific classifications etc.	Short phrases to annotate technique and design features	Balanced arguments that weigh up competing claims	Common use of graphs and diagrams to represent human and physical geography
Strong verbs to recount experimental write-up e.g. 'pour', 'put'	Adverbs and adjectives to convey artistic technique with precision	Adjectives to convey extent of a change e.g. 'critical' and 'insignificant'	Strong verbs to describe geographical phenomena clearly e.g. 'Rock armour *protects*...'

These pen portraits and simple summaries of writing in some subject disciplines only touch the surface of the writing demands faced by pupils from year 3 to year 13. Effectively, it is the opening of a dialogue for teachers to continue rather than a summary of established 'answers'. Each teacher brings their expertise in subject domains, writing, and their pupils (young or old) – but time and professional collaboration is likely needed to turn such expertise into action when it comes to disciplinary writing.

Teachers can start by reading and collating the best writing in each subject domain – identifying examples of different writing types and moves. We can then discuss and share how best to map the writing moves of each subject discipline into a manageable curriculum sequence.

And so, we return to the 'unattainable, mysterious tacit code' of writing in the classroom. It needn't be unattainable. It needn't be mysterious. It needn't be tacit. We can teach the code for every subject discipline, so that we begin to close the writing gap in every classroom.

IN SHORT ...

- For too many pupils, accessing the academic language of the curriculum is an 'unattainable' and 'mysterious' code. Teachers can use disciplinary literacy to reveal the subtle code of each and every subject discipline.
- As pupils move through school, writing becomes more sophisticated and subject specific. 'Disciplinary literacy' describes the common writing moves in every subject, but also the specialist 'branching off' where 'writing like a scientist' can be defined, practised, and understood.

- Subjects like art and science may write in concise and precise phrases. Extended writing is likely to be rare. And yet, even the use of annotations or single-sentence scientific definitions needs teaching, modelling and considerable practice.
- Teachers need to work collaboratively to identify, plan, and teach the writing in each discipline.

Notes

1 Lampi, J. P., & Reynolds, T. (2018). Connecting practice and research: From tacit to explicit disciplinary writing instruction. *Journal of Developmental Education*, *41*(2), Winter 2018.

2 Schleppegrell, M. J. (2004). *The language of schooling: A functional linguistics perspective*. London: Lawrence Erlbaum Associates Publishers.

3 Dunn, C., Holmes, D., & Cowling, D. (2016). *GCSE Geography Edexcel B Student Book*. OUP Oxford, UK Edition. Oxford: Oxford University Press.

4 Rundell, K. (2017). *The Explorer*. London: Bloomsbury.

5 Education Endowment Foundation. (2019). *Improving literacy in secondary school guidance report*. London: Education Endowment Foundation.

6 Halliday, M. A. K., edited by Webster, J. J. (2004). *The language of science*. London: Continuum.

7 Fang, Zhihui. (2021). *Demystifying academic writing*. 10.4324/9781003131618.

8 AQA (2019). GCSE Chemistry, 8462/1F: Paper 1 – Foundation Report on the Examination. Retrieved from: https://filestore.aqa.org.uk/sample-papers-and-mark-schemes/2019/june/AQA-84621F-WRE-JUN19.PDF.

9 Walker, R. (2018). Sentences and the web of knowledge. Retrieved from: https://rosalindwalker.wordpress.com/2018/10/17/sentences-and-the-web-of-knowledge/.

10 VanSledright, B. (2012). Learning with texts in history. In T. L. Jetton, & C. Shanahan (Eds.), *Adolescent literacy in*

the academic disciplines: General principles and practical strategies (pp. 199–226). New York: The Guilford Press.

11 Coffin, C. (2006). Learning the language of school history: the role of linguistics in mapping the writing demands of the secondary school curriculum. *Journal of Curriculum Studies, 38*(4), 413-429.

12 Carroll, J. A. (2016). The whole point of the thing: how nominalisation might develop students' written causal arguments. *Teaching History, 162,* 16–24, The Historical Association.

13 Ibid.

14 Jenner, T. (2019). Making reading routine: helping Key Stage 3 pupils to become regular readers of historical scholarship. *Teaching History, 174,* March 2019, The Historical Association.

15 Simmons, M. (2016). Developing written answers. *Teaching Geography, 41*(2), Focus on making progress (Summer 2016), 66–67, Geographical Association.

16 Ibid.

7 Practical strategies

Where do we start with practical strategies for teaching writing?

We know that writing is a not-so-simple task, and one that becomes increasingly more sophisticated and more subject specific as pupils move through school. We know that pupils routinely enact a multitude of writing moves, so we cannot address them all at the same time, or in an easy, formulaic sequence.

There are no gaping windows in the school timetable for additional teaching. And yet, there are lots of meaningful choices to be made to better refine the writing habits and practices of pupils every school day.

The secret to a practical, and pragmatic, approach to teaching writing is to seize the countless small opportunities to integrate it into our existing practice. Just as for expert professional writers, it will be a case of refined edits and subtle revisions to how writing is taught, not some revolutionary new approach or paid-for product, that will close the writing gap.

DOI: 10.4324/9781003179962-7

Practical strategies to...write about what you read

Reading and writing are two sides of the same coin. They prove to be complementary and overlapping skills, with one enhancing the other.[1] Writing well about your local area in year 3 requires lots of reading about people and places, their history and development. Writing poetry in year 9 English is almost always informed by reading and talking about a wide array of poems, their forms, and language choices.

Reading offers vital material for writing, whilst writing about what you read helps consolidate and enhance what you read.[2] At its simplest, writing about what you read makes you think harder and better organise your thinking. Though pupils seemingly do this a lot, they may do so inconsistently or inefficiently, and so precise, practical strategies prove a useful aid.

Effective ways to use writing to enhance pupils' understanding of what has been read could include:

- **Anchor points**. When pupils are reading texts in class, from textbooks to timeless classics, they are grappling with comprehending what they read. It is understandable that pupils may not notice the academic codes that are playing out before them. It therefore helps pupils to explicitly identify anchor points in the text – to stop, reflect and write about what they have read. Modelling predetermined stopping points, thereby chunking down the process, can be a strategy that pupils begin to use independently, such as when they are writing about a topic they have researched for homework.
- **Style stops**. The notion of stopping, reflecting, and writing about what has been read extends to identifying the style and academic code of the text. We can

once more model explicit style stops, whereat pupils can identify the writerly moves being exercised in the text. For example, pupils could be asked to identify the imagery used in an unseen poem in English or the use of tentative language in an account summarising World War One in a history lesson.

- **Stand out sentences**. A helpful way to draw out the style *and* substance of a text being read in the classroom is to ask pupils to identify stand out sentences. This could include a sentence that is the most compelling in an argument, the most important in an explanation, or the most evocative line in a poem. Writing about these sentences, along with discussion and debate, can make the all-too-tacit code of effective writing visible to pupils. A related benefit is that pupils go on to imitate such sentences in their own writing.
- **Gist sentences**. The strategy of summarising what has been read is a common one, but we can make assumptions that pupils always do this well.[3] We should be explicit that skimming a text and writing sentences about the gist (the key information, argument, or style features of a given text) when we read is a helpful record to aid understanding and remembering. For example, we can model a good gist sentence when reading about synagogues in religious education: 'Synagogues are the main place of worship for Jewish people' (key features: Ark, featuring Torah Scrolls; bimah; Siddur).
- **Connect, compare, or challenge**. Pupils need to be supported to make explicit links between different texts that they have read. For instance, when reading about X, they may not remember to make the connection with Y. Novice writers need help to activate their knowledge of different texts. Nudging pupils to write about text connections in their writing – such as comparing poems

in English, or comparing different descriptions of kingdoms of life in biology – can elicit helpful comparisons, points of contrast, or even challenges to a given text. Put simply, after reading we ask pupils to respond with the choice to connect, compare, or challenge.

Practical strategies to…improve pupils' note-taking

Pupils everywhere take lots of notes. Some notes are reliant upon the written word, some are predominantly visual; some notes are highly organised into hierarchies, some are quick and messy; some notes are recorded digitally, some are composed by hand. But what approaches to note-taking are likely to prove most effective?

It will not surprise you when I state that structuring and scaffolding note-taking is most likely to benefit pupils, from novice to expert. Making strategic notes, with effective guidance, ensures pupils think hard about what they have read, as well as translate, organise, and distil their understanding. Here are some evidence-informed approaches to notetaking:

- **The Cornell note-taking method**. This is one of the most popular approaches to strategic note-taking. Named after the US university, the method was devised in the 1950s by Professor Walter Pauk. Devised for students to make notes in lectures, it is a small step to using it to organise notes on a text you have read. It doesn't simply prompt pupils to write notes verbatim – it ensures that they isolate key words, record reflective questions, and compose a succinct summary. Crucially, the summary column demands a prioritisation of the material, which ensures pupils must do the tricky thinking of distilling the most essential information (see Figure 7.1).

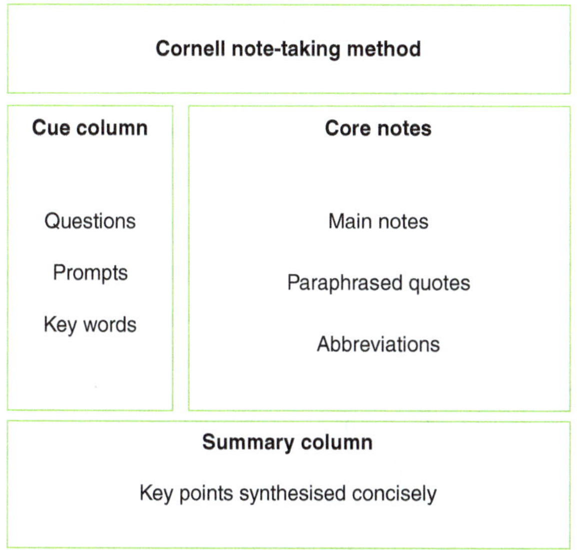

Figure 7.1 The Cornell note-taking method

- **Guided note-taking**. Guided note-taking can include pre-prepared structured documents (both print and digital), step-by-step prompts and guidance from the teacher, or a combination of both approaches to structuring written notes. For novice or struggling writers, there are gains to be made from modelling and structuring notes in guided steps. For example, using smaller spaces and boxes to respond to prompts can nudge pupils to be more concise and to practise simplifying syntax or using abbreviations and codes.
- **Paraphrasing practice**. One of the common moves when note-taking or writing academic essays is the act of paraphrasing, that is, the restating of information or ideas from a text in your own words. Many pupils can do this from a young age without realising it. It should be a writing move that is practised – with pupils

understanding the difference between a near copy, minimal revision, moderate revision, and substantial revision.[4] To do so, pupils should be guided to directly copy quotes from texts, all the way to concise paraphrasing, and evaluating the effects of these different moves. For example:

1. *Direct quote*: 'Most people who bother with the matter at all would admit that the English language is in a bad way, but it is generally assumed that we cannot by conscious action do anything about it.'
   George Orwell, *Politics and the English Language*
2. *Embedded quote*: 'Orwell argues that "the English language is in a bad way" and that we cannot consciously "do anything about it".'
3. *Paraphrasing*: 'Orwell argues that the English language is in decline and beyond our ability to change it with intent.'

- **Big questions**. It is not enough for pupils to copy notes from what they read, or from teacher explanations. They need to do something with their notes and elaborate on their thinking. One strategy to do so is to encourage pupils to generate big questions as a result of their note-taking. Each pupil could generate a big question, before discussing it, attempting to answer the question, and so on. It also offers a useful retrieval activity to revisit the question.
- **Read, collaborate, and revise**. Pupils can gain from explicit structuring of notes, modelling moves like paraphrasing, and activating peers to pose discussion points and add to their note-taking. The 'read, collaborate, and revise' approach simply gets peers to collaborate in a structured fashion, first by reading one another's notes, then discussing their relative merits – differences, similarities, strengths, omissions etc. – before finally

offering feedback to revise their notes, with the aim of maximising the quality of the notes. There is of course has the additional benefit of reading multiple notes on the same content.

Practical strategies to...model writing

Modelling writing is one of the oldest moves in the history of teaching writing. Aristotle, in his *Poetics*, stated that imitation is natural to man, and in every classroom since it has proven to be an essential part of the teacher's repertoire. Though we have been doing it since writing instruction began, it can still prove an elusive, tricky act to master.

Whether it is reading an exemplary text or observing the teacher model an example 'live', the notion of effective modelling is to expose pupils to excellent ideas, as well as exemplify the thinking processes that led to the writing moves being made (described as a 'Think aloud'). There are a lot of potential variations for modelling writing:

Modelling approach	Potential benefits	Potential limitations
100% teacher modelling *Live modelling, undertaken wholly by the teacher, with no direct pupil input. It typically includes a teacher 'Think aloud', where they verbalise the thinking behind their writing moves as they enact them.*	This approach allows for pupils to devote all their mental effort to engaging with the ideas during composition, along with the moves being made by teachers at each step of the writing process.	The observation of the teacher demands concentration, and potential passivity from pupils may see them not fully engage with the writing process. Pupils may not be able to make the jump to enacting the moves independently.

(*continued*)

Modelling approach	Potential benefits	Potential limitations
Whole class shared modelling *Teacher-led modelling of writing to the group, but interactive, with pupils contributing ideas, making suggested edits etc.*	This approach allows for pupils to be led by an expert, and so their ideas can be scaffolded, with discussion and shared insights aiding novice pupils who may struggle to produce complex writing independently.	The approach can be highly demanding and induce split attention, between following the teacher's moves, contributing ideas, and listening to peers.
Small group shared modelling *An interactive approach led by the teacher, but with a smaller group to allow for more detailed interactions and support of individuals.*	This approach offers the teacher opportunity to provide more individualised support for struggling writers. It offers a well-structured scaffold, whilst still ensuring pupils generate their own ideas and writing moves.	This approach, by its nature, only reaches a small group, so it may have tricky implications for classroom management and the monitoring of the whole group, or require additional teaching time.

Modelling approach	Potential benefits	Potential limitations
Partial modelling *An interactive approach led by a teacher, who initiates a writing model but then hands over responsibility for pupils to continue the writing task.*	This approach offers the benefit of pupils being able to devote attention to the teacher's expert writing moves, but then goes on to undertake scaffolded practice of their own writing moves.	This approach may encourage a reliance on teacher planning and initiating writing, and so potentially stunt independent writing. Pupils could struggle to sustain the model.
Modelling of examples and non-examples *The teacher models effective writing by sharing expert examples and flawed exemplars by way of comparison.*	Pupils can benefit from the contrast of examples and non-examples, as they are exposed to excellent models but can also critique flawed examples that expose common errors or misconceptions.	The selection, identification, or production of multiple examples can require intensive planning. Additionally, pupils may not be able to distinguish the errors in the non-examples, so new misconceptions may be formed.

(*continued*)

Modelling approach	Potential benefits	Potential limitations
Peer modelling *Pupils write collaboratively, mostly independent of the teacher.*	This collaborative approach can encourage writing independence, whilst still having the supportive input of one or more peers. It can develop independent writing.	Even in collaboration, pupils may lack the knowledge to write effectively. Also, effective peer working can be demanding and require significant scaffolding and skilled classroom management.

There is little evidence that any single modelling approach is best. As such, teacher judgement needs to be exercised to decide upon the degree of modelling and scaffolding required. The prior knowledge and relative expertise of pupils, along with the degree of complexity of the writing task, are clearly significant in determining what approach to select.

The role of the 'gradual release of responsibility' that is baked into the modelling process is commonly characterised simply by the process: 'I do > we do > you do'. And yet, no simple three-step formula captures the complexity of decision-making that attends teacher modelling. A variety of approaches may need to be deployed over time and intelligently adapted:

- **Goldilocks mentor texts**. Mentor texts describe good examples of writing, which offer pupils ideas and exhibit the demands of the writing task.[5] There needs to be careful teacher judgement about whether expert models by professional authors are preferable to more accessible examples from peers. We can apply the Goldilocks principle to mentor texts: they should not be too easy nor too hard – but just right. For example, it may mean the difference between reading an expert article from a historian on the causes of World War One or a past essay from a pupil. Of course, you can usefully deploy both to good effect.

- **Compare and contrast**. Building on the Goldilocks approach, teachers can avoid always choosing excellent exemplars that pupils may feel are beyond them. There is some evidence to indicate it is more effective to get pupils to compare excellent models with flawed examples[6] (also commonly described as 'examples' and 'non-examples'). This can have the added benefit of exposing pupils to more examples that build their background knowledge of a topic or writing genre.
- **Reverse engineering writing models**. It can be useful to use mentor texts with pupils, but to effectively reverse engineer plans for it. For example, the teacher takes a skilled narrative description of the Great Fire of London and models a plausible paragraph plan that isolates some of the essential moves of the writer. This approach can have the double benefit of modelling an excellent example whilst additionally modelling crucial planning processes.
- **Demonstration > prompt > practice**. Professor Tim Shanahan, a literacy expert from the US, has helpfully described a process for modelling.[7] He first describes a manageable *demonstration* that doesn't overwhelm pupils, such as how to write a right branching sentence, then clearly *prompting* about what features of the demonstration to notice, before quickly getting pupils to *practise* the writing move themselves.

- **Mid-task modelling**. A common teaching technique is to select mentor texts before pupils engage in their own writing. An issue with this approach is that pupils can often be too keen to closely imitate the mentor text. Delaying the introduction of a mentor text until the middle of a writing task, or at least after the planning has been undertaken, can reduce imitation whilst still exemplifying writerly moves, or offer stimulus to make some timely revisions and edits.

Practical strategies to…structure excellent arguments

Writing to argue – whether that is an essay, a speech, or an article – is one of the most common writing types in every classroom at each key stage. We return to the roots of rhetoric and how the power of written arguments helped shape the laws and lives of ancient societies and endures in our classrooms and courtrooms to this day.

Fundamentally, effective arguments are founded on comprehensive and confident knowledge of a given topic of debate. No approach to planning or writing techniques can compensate for a substantial background knowledge deficit. And yet, if we combine building background knowledge with explicit teaching of how to skilfully assemble the structure of an argument, then we offer pupils of all ages the essential moves for writing excellent arguments.

It is helpful to make explicit that there are different types of argument. In history or religious education, an argument would likely expect 'balance', whereas in English or in politics, a more persuasive, one-sided approach may be permitted or actively encouraged. Both argument types are broadly parallel in structure, so they can be planned similarly:

A balanced argument	A persuasive argument
Introduction *e.g. explain the relevance of the topic and the competing claims in the debate*	**Introduction** *e.g. explain the importance of the topic and forcefully state your main claim*
Evidence supporting your argument *e.g. explain your position and pose evidence*	**Claims supporting your argument** *e.g. explain your position with emotive examples and evidence*
Evidence challenging your argument *e.g. explain counter arguments with evidence*	**Claims supporting your argument** *e.g. further exemplification that anticipates common counter arguments*
Weighing up competing claims *e.g. balance competing positions and claims*	**Refuting challenges to your argument** *e.g. explain challenges to your position with strong refutation*
Conclusion *e.g. summarise both sides of the argument and restate your reasoned position*	**Conclusion** *e.g. end argument with rhetorical force, such as personal example*

Once we support pupils to recognise structural differences between a balanced argument and a more persuasive, rhetorical stance, then we can be specific about stylistic differences. Clearly, a balanced argument may use more tentative language, compared to the emotive language that intensifies feeling in a persuasive argument ('utterly dreadful' and 'beyond comprehension').

Practical strategies

Here are some practical strategies to structure argument writing:

- **Argument stacking**. Pupils need to generate ideas and claims for their argument. It is often a strategy that is highly engaging for pupils (who doesn't love a good argument?), but too often pupils fail to balance their argument. One practical strategy to both generate and plan arguments is to practise argument stacking. Consider the classic weighing scales of Lady Justice. Pupils need to stack up claims and ideas for and against a given argument (a simple weighing scales graphic organiser can offer a visual record for pupils).
- **Anticipating your ideal audience**. You cannot consider an effective argument without a well-developed sense of your audience. Alongside generating ideas and claims for a given debate, pupils need to be encouraged to create a caricature of their ideal audience. What beliefs, assumptions, and background knowledge would they possess? Would they be convinced by evidence and statistics? Would they be engaged by humour or personal stories? Would they expect a balanced view, or something more partisan and persuasive?
- **The subjectivity spectrum**. To write arguments, pupils need to ideally read and hear an array of effective worked examples. Pupils can better understand the differences between a balanced argument and a more persuasive stance by exploring how they deploy a scientific and objective style or a slanted and subjective position, on a spectrum. It could be a comparison between using facts and statistics and providing a moving personal example. By distilling the features of multiple examples, pupils are less likely to borrow too heavily from a single example, so their writing moves become

more nuanced. We can simplify the process further by simply comparing sentences and their argument styles. Take this pair of sentences arguing for the preservation of the Amazon rainforest:

1. *Balanced argument style*: The Amazon rainforest provides essential natural, cultural, and economic functions.
2. *Persuasive style:* The Amazon rainforest biome is shrinking, depriving Mother Nature of a vital organ, and threatening the health of countless ecosystems.

- **Sequencing topic sentences**. Topic sentences effectively signpost your main arguments. They typically begin and frame each paragraph in an argument. To illustrate, if you were planning to write a persuasive argument to stop the deforestation of the Amazon in year 5, you may devise the following:
  1. Introduction: The Amazon, the world's largest rainforest, is home to millions of people and it is essential to the lives of billions.
  2. Paragraph 2: Deforestation is damaging the health of the Amazon.
  3. Paragraph 3: The health of the Amazon is vital when considering climate change.
  4. Paragraph 4: The deforestation of the Amazon does produce important farming and foods.
  5. Conclusion: A quarter of the Amazon rainforest biome is predicted to be destroyed in the next decade.

  It is a helpful planning approach to single out clear and cogent topic sentences. They offer a planning spine that can be discussed, revised, and edited, before the more complex job of completing a full draft.
- **Ordered argument planning**. For thousands of years, since the birth of rhetoric, writers have been organising

effective arguments. We can embed the strategies into the following six-step planning sequence for excellent arguments:

1. *Summarise* (summarise your argument in a single sentence)
2. *Generate* (get argument stacking, sourcing evidence, examples, and ideas)
3. *Organise* (sequence your argument in a paragraph plan – identifying thesis statements)
4. *Elaborate* (add to ideas and flesh out your paragraph plan – adding facts, statistics, judgements, personal testimony, ideas, observations, and similar)
5. *Synthesise* (review your plan with your ideal audience in mind, check the balance of your argument)
6. *Scrutinise* (check over your planning for inaccuracies or errors)

   Note: If you want to keep planning scrutiny simple, you can use the SCAN strategy (does it make **s**ense? Is it **c**onnected to my belief? Can I **a**dd more? **N**ote errors[8]).

Practical strategies to...plan narrative writing

Story writing is perhaps the most popular writing of all, holding a privileged place at the heart of our culture. When we read stories we help unlock imagined worlds for our pupils, whilst helping them absorb their rhythms, characters, problems and resolutions.

There is no straightforward formula for writing great stories, though thousands of people have attempted to write books on the subject. Happily though, helping novice pupils to better plan their ideas when undertaking narrative writing is a goal that is within our grasp.

Of course, guidance for a novelist writing a 300-page tome is distinctly different to school writing, which expects pupils to crystallise and amplify narrative moves in a mere few hundred words. As such, we should plan with an eye for what we can call 'compact narrative writing', which invariably describes shortened narratives focused on fewer events or shifts in time or setting.

Here are some practical strategies for planning 'compact narrative writing':

- **Five-act structure and Freytag's Pyramid**. We can trace story structures all the way back to Aristotle and ancient Greece. The five-act dramatic structure has been passed on, from Sophocles to Shakespeare, but it is also hidden in plain view in countless Hollywood blockbusters and great novels. The German dramatist, Gustav Freytag, offered us a helpful pyramid structure to convey the five-act structure (see Figure 7.2).

Here is the pyramid applied to Shakespeare's 'Romeo and Juliet':

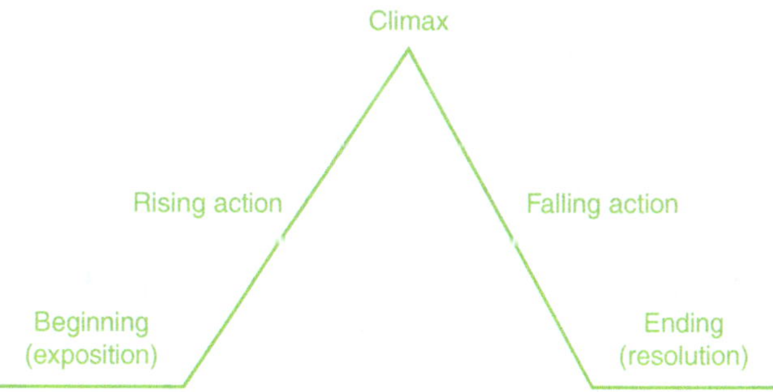

Figure 7.2 Freytag's Pyramid

1. **Beginning/exposition**: the prologue and the family feud introduce the tragic setting of Renaissance Verona.
2. **Rising action**: Romeo and Juliet meet and fall in love
3. **Climax**: Tybalt kills Mercutio and Romeo kills Tybalt in a fit of vengeance.
4. **Falling action**: Juliet plots with the Friar as she resists being married off to Paris.
5. **Ending/resolution**: Juliet and Romeo kill themselves in a scene of tragic miscommunication.

Freytag's pyramid structure has been recast as a mountain, a map, and a volcano, but the principle remains the same: a plot is artfully constructed with the audience's expectations in mind.

By establishing a common story structure, pupils can use it to carry their audience along with them, or artfully break from the norm to excite and surprise. Even in 'compact narrative writing', the narrative arc of rising to a climax, before falling to a resolution, can prove helpful and useful as a planning structure.

- **Story timeline sketching**. Pupils typically need support to structure their narrative writing with a consideration of pacing their narrative, and, in practical terms, of just how much writing that will take. For example, if a pupil has scope for a narrative of around 1000 words (more commonly in Key Stage 2 and beyond), then they must carefully consider how much depth is required to introduce their characters and setting (the exposition). And yet, many pupils fail to take this practical step. If they have a pyramid plan, or similar, they can roughly sketch the projected pacing of a story (see Figure 7.3).
- **Seven Basic Plots**. In terms of narrative structure, shining a light on genre, like horror and mystery stories,

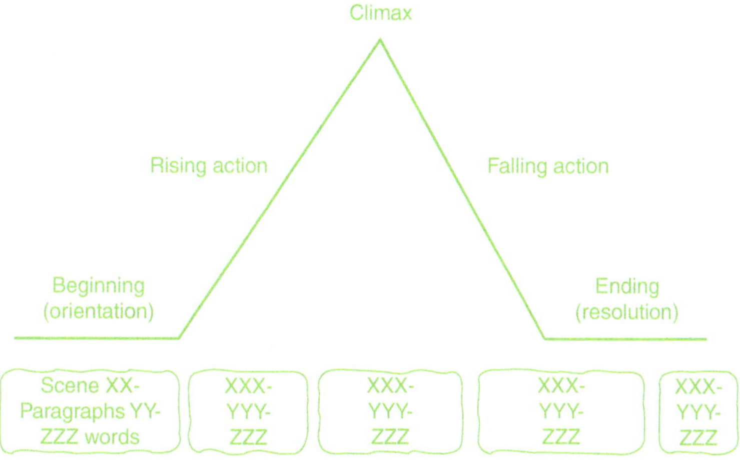

Figure 7.3 Story timeline sketch

is a common approach to teaching narrative writing. Focusing on genre elements offers pupils crucial mentor texts and a range of narrative structures and ideas to imitate and manipulate. English author Christopher Booker, in his seminal book *The Seven Basic Plots*,[9] went one further in revealing how all stories fall into seven archetypal plots:

1. **Overcoming the monster**. A hero defeats an evil force (not always an actual monster) – think *Beowulf* or *Dracula*.
2. **Rags to riches**. Insignificant and poor, then elevated to exceptional – think *Great Expectations* or *The Great Gatsby*.
3. **The quest**. Hero overcomes an obstacle-laden journey – think *Lord of the Rings* or *The Explorer*.
4. **Voyage and return**. Hero travels from the familiar to a strange world, before a safe return – think *Alice in Wonderland* or *The Wonderful Wizard of Oz*.

5. **Comedy**. A hero and heroine overcome confusion, and worse, before uniting happily ever after – think *Pride and Prejudice* or *The Princess Bride*.
6. **Tragedy**. Flawed choices are taken by characters leading to destructive ends – think *Macbeth* or *1984*.
7. **Rebirth**. A troublesome character gains renewal and redemption – think *A Christmas Carol* or *Beauty and the Beast*.

Booker offers common stages for each plot, but the real magic is discussing, comparing, and debating examples – their plots and patterns – so that pupils have narrative structures they can draw upon.

- **Casting characters**. Predictable plot patterns can be matched by archetypal characters that prove familiar to the reader. When pupils explore and compare common character archetypes, it offers them more ideas and templates for their plans. There are many categories for character archetypes (such as Vladimir Propp's influential fairy-tale archetypes), but just some include:
    1. **The villain** – think Professor Moriarty or Voldemort.
    2. **The hero** – think Offred or Katniss Everdeen.
    3. **The helper** – think Samwise Gamgee or Hermione Granger.
    4. **The mentor** – think Gandalf or the Fairy Godmother.
    5. **The false hero** – think Draco Malfoy or Jay Gatsby.
    6. **The princess** – think Rapunzel or Eliza Doolittle.

    These character types offer stimulus for pupils and their own characters. Such examples and conventions can be reinforced, reversed, or wholeheartedly rejected.
- **The writing conference**. A practical process for teachers to support pupils' planning – likely individually, but sometimes in small groups – is to hold a writing conference.[10] This teaching strategy describes

the structured conversation between pupils and their teachers. Pupils get to explain their narrative writing choices and receive feedback to guide their planning, drafting, editing, and revising. Feedback can be targeted – for instance, a focus on plot structure, or the use of vocabulary and imagery – so that several pupils can benefit from the approach.

Practical strategies to…improve paragraphing

Sentences may be the essential unit when it comes to teaching pupils to write, but perfecting the paragraph runs a close second. A significant proportion of planning – whether for an essay, a narrative, or a lengthy exam question – can be seen through the lens of paragraph structures.

Trying to define and impose hard and fast rules for paragraphing is predictably troublesome. In newspaper articles, paragraphs can commonly be a sentence or two in length (given the need for 'white space' on the page to aid readability), whereas in an academic essay a paragraph is expected to develop arguments with evidence that can require ten times the number of sentences in a pithy news report.

Many informational texts and essays begin paragraphs with a topic sentence – an introductory sentence that typically summarises the topic of that paragraph – but this practice can vary from text to text.

How long is a paragraph...well, how long is any piece of prose? Should a paragraph be focused on a single idea or topic? Yes, of course...except when it doesn't. For novice pupils, advice that is basically 'anything goes' isn't very helpful, so we may seek out meaningful principles and practices to cohere paragraphs, linking them up effectively and sequencing them fluently.

Practical strategies

Here are some practical strategies to help improve pupils' paragraphing:

- **What's the big idea?** At the planning stage, or when revising extended writing which contains a chain of paragraphs, pupils need to be able to talk about their choices. We can ask pupils 'What's the big idea?' of a particular paragraph. Of course, their topic sentences *should* signpost this clearly. Similarly, when revising a paragraph, you can pose the same question so that pupils can evaluate how effective they have been in explaining or arguing for that big idea. They can be prompted to check whether they have mobilised evidence, exemplification, and apt vocabulary, to communicate that big idea.
- **Paragraph shrinking**. Another angle on identifying the essential information for a given paragraph is to reverse the writing process. Once pupils have written a paragraph, or paragraphs, if they can shrink each one down to a few words, or a sentence, they can summarise it, and thereby judge their effectiveness in communicating their ideas. In year 8 writing explaining sustainable ecosystems, such paragraph shrinking offers a ready-made topic sentence.
- **Working on 'white space'**. With so much writing being read online, writing has shifted in many contexts to shorter, more readable paragraphs. A single-sentence paragraph can be striking, offering rhetorical force, when you write with white space in mind. Read an online TES article, or similar, and you will recognise that professional writers use white space to aid readability. White space is not new to writing. English teacher and school leader Phil Stock argues that white space is "essential in the writing (and reading) of

poetry"[11] – an ancient form of writing. And so, working on white space, and making this necessity explicit to pupils, proves helpful when paragraphing.

- **Traffic light paragraphing**. One of the simpler ways to evaluate the clarity and cohesion of a single paragraph is to apply a traffic light system to it. That is to say, the *introduction* – or topic sentence – is identified in green, the *body* of the paragraph is highlighted in amber and, finally, the *conclusion* of the paragraph is highlighted in red. Once identified, these common three parts of a paragraph can be evaluated more easily. *Does this introduction clearly signpost the topic or argument? Does the body offer adequate evidence and examples? Does the conclusion synthesise the arguments or the range of examples?*
- **Graphic organisers**. An enduring and popular approach to planning and organising ideas in writing is to apply a range of graphic organisers. Each graphic design can be matched to the writing content and structure, and they can match particularly well with devising a paragraph structure. Some examples include:
  1. **T diagram**: useful for balanced argument writing, balancing up opposing claims (see Figure 7.4)
  2. **Concept map**: useful for informational writing, such as a case study explaining a specific place in geography, given it prompts relationships between ideas and concepts (see Figure 7.5)
  3. **Fishbone diagram**: useful for developed arguments that display cause and effect, such as a history essay exploring the causes of World War One (see Figure 7.6)
  4. **Persuasion map**: useful for planning and organising arguments and persuasive writing (see Figure 7.7).

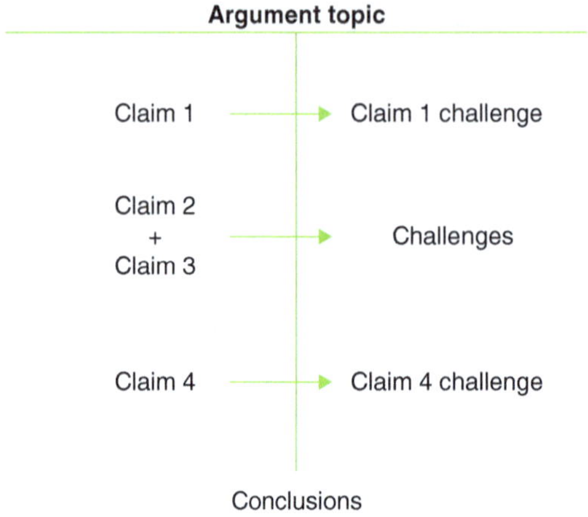

Figure 7.4 T diagram

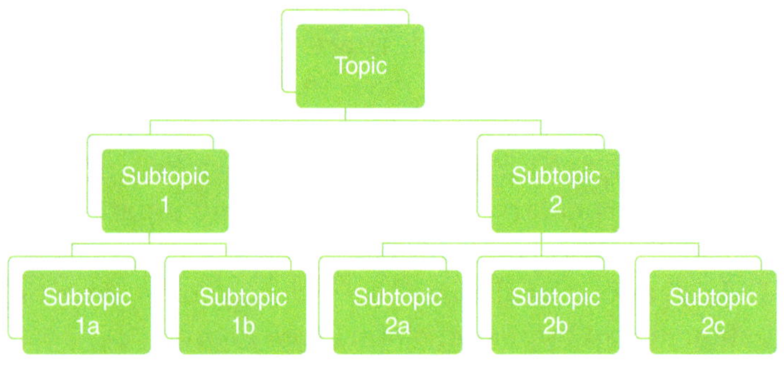

Figure 7.5 Concept map

Practical strategies to…practise structured talk to enhance writing

From the age of the ancients, writing, talk and speech have been inextricably linked to writing in the classroom. Quintilian and Aristotle simply wouldn't have separated out speech and writing. And still today, throughout the writing process and when undertaking writing practice, teacher–pupil talk and peer dialogue prove essential.

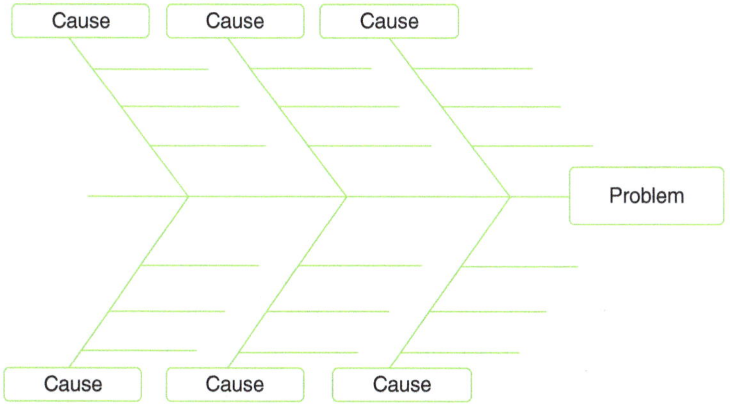

Figure 7.6 Fishbone diagram

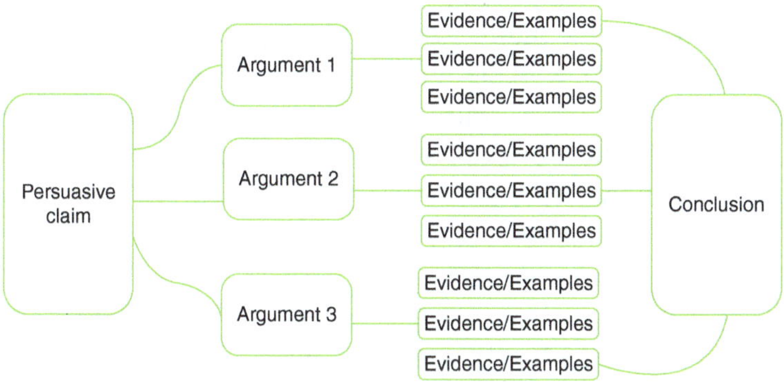

Figure 7.7 Persuasion map

Given the array of complex moves in every writing task, exploring ideas verbally proves a vital prerequisite for writing success. Research evidence repeatedly backs up this case. For example, written arguments can prove more effective when dialogue and interactions exploring that argument occur.[12]

Structured talk helps generate and elaborate on ideas *before* writing and offers challenge and clarification *during* writing along with reflection and refinement *after* writing. Here are some practical strategies for using structured talk to enhance writing:

Before writing:

- **I say, you say**. Pupils being able to generate a range of ideas, drawing upon a wealth of background knowledge, is a determining factor in writing quality. It can help to activate that knowledge by getting pupils to explicitly consider both their audience and any additional viewpoints or arguments on a given topic. The simple notion of 'you say' is to stimulate a response to a range of views and the reception of a given piece of writing. Of course, this makes this approach something that works well in well-structured small groups. By explicitly sharing ideas and collaborating at the planning stage, we invariably support pupils to generate a richer plan for their writing.
- **Planning partners**. A focused collaborative activity in the planning stage is to assign planning partners. This approach can be explicitly structured so that pupils independently devise their plan, then their partner annotates their planning, with additional ideas and questions, before discussing those insights. This crafted collaboration can helpfully slow down pupils and expose them to contradictory opinions and once more expose them to the crucial notion of writing for a specific, and real, audience.

During writing:

- **Stop, elaborate and listen**. Pupils in the middle of writing can find it hard to stop, step out of the act of

drafting, and reflect upon their progress so far. This approach is a method to slow pupils down and to make explicit those key writing processes of revising, editing, and evaluating their writing. Put simply, they stop their writing (this can be at a set time or at a point in writing, e.g. after paragraph X or at the end of section Y), then they are expected to read and discuss their writing so far with a peer, or the teacher, before listening to feedback targeted on revisions and editing. This process invariably needs modelling from the teacher. It makes for writing that is slower but usually more successful.
- **Add, remove, refine**. Another approach to stopping and revising in the middle of the act of writing (particularly extended writing) is the prompt to 'add, remove, refine'. It does what it says on the tin: pupils are to revise a specific portion of their writing with an awareness that editing may include sentence expansion, shrinking, or adaptation for sense. Pupils can be reluctant to stop writing, and particularly to chop out any substandard or extraneous writing, so this element requires sensitive modelling and guidance.

After writing:

- **Author's chair**.[13] This approach sees pupils read some, or all, of their writing to the class. The teacher poses carefully crafted feedback that highlights successful elements of the writing, whilst also sensitively nudging potential tweaks and revisions, before pupils take on the role of the audience offering feedback.
- **Critique**. Another approach to focusing upon revising, editing, and evaluating writing (taking care to emphasise pupils' writing strengths rather than criticism) with sensitive feedback is the 'critique' method. Devised by

US educator, Ron Berger, it specifies three elements of verbal feedback:

1. **Be specific**: focus on writing elements, e.g. 'I like the way you use sentence signposts to make the process really clear.'
2. **Be kind**: focus on strengths, e.g. 'I enjoyed how you kept directly addressing the reader and how this created a friendly, personal tone.'
3. **Be helpful**: focus on offering precise, productive feedback, e.g. 'Have you considered using rhetorical repetition – such as anaphora or asyndeton – to add some punch to the point about unsustainable damage to the Amazon?'

Practical strategies to…foster writing motivation

Trying to motivate pupils to write can be a mercurial and difficult process. We can miss the mark with motivation by trying to fuel pupils with praise or supplying them with empty truisms like 'everyone has a novel inside them'. Even well-meaning praise is quickly punctured when pupils struggle to compose a sentence with confidence.

There are a range of suggestions about what motivates pupils to write: some fruitful, some fanciful, and some which need unpicking. Here are some approaches that may bear fruit when trying to grow and sustain the motivation of pupils:

- **Start with success**. Puffed up praise fails, whereas experiencing writing success sustains.[14] When you can make a hundred moves with a sentence, an argument, or a story, you experience repeated success. When you write a great letter in the guise of Samuel Pepys as you learn about the Great Fire of London, you can better retain your knowledge of history, but just as importantly you can gain a sense of self-confidence in your ability as a writer.[15] The next historical recount you write can build on more confident foundations. Ron Berger captured it brilliantly when he stated: 'Once a student sees that he or she is capable of quality, of excellence, that student is never quite the same. There is a new self-image, a new notion of possibility.'[16]

- **Make it clear**. We can too often assume that pupils are lacking motivation to undertake their writing task, when they are actually struggling with a lack of clarity. If a pupil's writing is full of errors, is it because they are demotivated, or is it because they struggle with spelling, and more, and simply cannot manage to edit? Making a writing task clear is usually aided by multiple mentor texts and ample modelling, but also by isolating the key moves in the game in a manageable process. Repeatedly stating the aims of the writing task, along with generating checklists, can ensure greater clarity for pupils.
- **Harness the power of habit**. Writing is hard: it can tax your emotions and max out your working memory. And so, stopping, checking, revising, and editing – those key processes that lead to successful writing – all feel like arduous extras to many of our pupils. We can motivate pupils with *habitual goals*. For example, daily writing sprints could be accompanied by goals for both the timing and the legibility of their writing. *Classroom cues*[17] can help trigger good habits and therefore build success that fosters motivation. For instance, sentence signposting or Goldilocks mentor texts could be referenced visibly on a classroom display.
- **Make it real**. We can make the act of writing more meaningful and motivating by making it real. It isn't always viable to have an actual audience (making notes

about covalent bonding in GCSE chemistry lacks any real audience compared to the experience of sending a persuasive letter to the Prime Minister), but we can ensure that awareness of real audiences occurs when it is meaningful. Additionally, mobilising peers as a supporting audience for one another, with a well-structured feedback process, can prove a helpful proxy for that all-important sense of an audience.

- **Make it meaningful**. The motivation of pupils can wax and wane. It is a reality shared by every teacher and pupil that some writing tasks can be intrinsically interesting, whereas others can prove rather boring! We can relate some writing activities to our pupils' lives and experiences, drawing upon their personal funds of knowledge[18] – their family and personal passions – to generate meaningful writing tasks. For more teacher-focused writing, like examination responses or class notes, notions of value derive from the pupils' trust and respect for the teacher. One aspect of that may be the teacher offering consistent and kind feedback.
- **Consider choice and autonomy**. The school day can be a fast-moving train for many pupils. They have few choices and are hurtling along at great speed. When it comes to embedding choice in school writing, there are practical boundaries, but there are countless opportunities to generate motivation via pupil choice too. Big choices may include having completely open choice for creative writing in English. A small choice may include pupils deciding which planning strategy to use to shape their writing about a great artist in year 5 art. Choice needs to be carefully calibrated with expertise. For novice pupils, too much choice can be overwhelming, but for expert pupils such autonomy can be highly motivating.

The writing gap can seem so pressing for our struggling pupils that we feel compelled to get started and try an array of new strategies right away. And yet, integrating even one new strategy within our established habits and routines always proves more challenging than we might at first expect. Instead, we should be cautious but positive, identifying a small number of changes that we can develop and sustain in our classroom routines.

We should consider the following questions when deciding what practical strategies we should deploy:

- What small number of strategies can I feasibly integrate into my habitual practice?
- What writing strategies will I keep using in my teaching, but deploy differently?
- What approaches to teaching writing will I use less of or stop using?
- How will I know these strategies are having a positive impact?

Notes

1 Education Endowment Foundation. (2019). *Improving literacy in secondary school guidance report.* London: Education Endowment Foundation.

2 Graham, S., & Hebert, M. A. (2010). *Writing to read: Evidence for how writing can improve reading.* A Carnegie Corporation Time to Act Report. Washington, DC: Alliance for Excellent Education.

3 Dunlosky, J., Rawson, K. A., Marsh, E. J., Nathan, M. J., & Willingham, D. T. (2013). Improving students' learning with effective learning techniques: Promising directions from cognitive and educational psychology. *Psychological Science in the Public Interest, 14,* 4–58. http://doi.org/10.1177/1529100612453266.

4 Keck, C. (2006). The use of paraphrase in summary writing: A comparison of L1 and L2 writers. *Journal of Second Language Writing, 15*(4), 261–278.

5 Graham, S., Harris, K. R., & Chambers, A. B. (2016). Evidence-based practice and writing instruction: A review of reviews. In C. A. MacArthur, S. Graham, & J. Fitzgerald (Eds.), *Handbook of writing research* (pp. 211–226). New York: The Guilford Press.

6 Rohbanfard, H., & Proteau, L. (2011). Learning through observation: a combination of expert and novice models favors learning. *Experimental Brain Research, 215*, 183–197.

7 Shanahan, T. (2020). Does 'modeling' have a place in high quality literacy teaching? Retrieved from: https://shanahanonliteracy.com/blog/does-modeling-have-a-place-in-high-quality-literacy-teaching.

8 Graham, S., & MacArthur, C. (1988). Improving learning disabled students' skills at revising essays produced on a word processor: Self-instructional strategy training. *The Journal of Special Education, 22*(2), 133–152. https://doi.org/10.1177/002246698802200202.

9 Booker, C. (2005). *The seven basic plots: Why we tell stories.* London: Bloomsbury.

10 Graves, D. (1982). Six guideposts to a successful writing conference. *Learning, 11*(4), 76–77.

11 Stock, P. (2021, September 4). *Disciplinary Literacy.* researchED National Conference, London.

12 Hemberger, L., Kuhn, D., Matos, F., & Shi, Y. (2017). A dialogic path to evidence-based argumentative writing. *Journal of the Learning Sciences, 26*(4), 575–607. doi:10.1080/10508406.2017.1336714.

13 Graham et al. (2012). Teaching elementary students to be effective writers: A practice guide (NCEE 2012-4058). Washington, DC: National Centre for Education Evaluation and Regional Assistance, Institute of Education Sciences, US Department for Education. Retrieved from: http://ies.gove/ncee/wwc/publications_reviews.aspx#pubsearch.

14 Marsh, H. W., & Martin, A. J. (2011). Academic self-concept and academic achievement: Relations and causal ordering. *British Journal of Educational Psychology, 81*, 59–77. https://doi.org/10.1348/000709910X503501.

15 Pajares, F. (2003). Self-efficacy beliefs, motivation, and achievement in writing: A Review of the literature. *Reading & Writing Quarterly, 19*(2), 139–158. doi:10.1080/10573560308222.
16 Berger, R. (2003). *An ethic of excellence: Building a culture of craftsmanship with students.* New Hampshire: Heinemann Educational Books.
17 Fletcher-Wood, H. (2021). *Habits of success: Getting every student learning.* Oxon: Routledge.
18 Vélez-Ibáñez, C. G., & Greenberg, J. B. (1992). Formation and transformation of funds of knowledge among US Mexican households. *Anthropology & Education Quarterly, 23*(4), 313–335.

8 Next steps

Every teacher is a writer. Whether it is sending daily emails, drafting lesson plans, composing comments on pupils' writing, or even crafting novels in the far corners of evenings, teachers engage in the act of writing. But being an expert writer does not constitute the tricky job of teaching novice pupils how to write successfully.

We return once more to the estimated seven million adults in England who are considered to be 'functionally illiterate'. It is a statistic that is simply hard to fathom in real terms. If you are reading this book, not only are you not one of the seven million, but you are also unlikely to know many adults within the sobering statistic who struggle to read and write. It is no surprise – their voices commonly go unheard in professional circles. Their experience of school typically goes largely unwritten.

My father would likely be part of this faceless cast of millions who struggle to write. He follows the news each day, navigates the sports pages of the *Liverpool Echo*, and can hold a political debate with anyone. And yet, there have been countless times in my father's life when he couldn't exercise the vital power of writing. Perhaps it was an unsent message. Perhaps it was an unsent email of complaint or

 DOI: 10.4324/9781003179962-8

challenge to his boss. Perhaps it was an unsent job qualification form for a hoped-for new opportunity.

My father still got by without writing. Many pupils navigate the school day without writing skilfully too. They may get by, but it is a grim story of unwritten, quiet frustration. Frustration attends all aspects of the writing gap: the frustration that teachers face when they are unsure how to support a pupil who struggles to spell; the frustration a parent feels when faced with homework on SPaG that they are unable to decipher.

I am proud of all my father's successes. But I am frustrated that he left school unable to write confidently, along with all the limitations, challenges and missed opportunities in his life that he faced as a result.

Too often, we hear platitudes about equity in schools, or handwringing about abstract notions of social mobility. But what about practical solutions? You can shrink the massive, amorphous challenge of poor literacy into manageable and meaningful goals and practical solutions. You can make a start on narrowing the gap for those pupils who will rely on the skill of writing to succeed in school.

In an age of mass writing unlike any other, every pupil leaving school as a confident, skilled writer should prove a priority that it is within our gift to address.

Assessing and addressing writing gaps

What do the literary classics *The Chronicles of Narnia, The Tale of Peter Rabbit, Lord of the Flies,* and *Gone with the Wind* have in common? They were all rejected by a myriad of potential publishers. Frankly, dear reader, judging writing can be damn hard.

Assessing the quality of writing can be a challenging task – whether it is a short answer in science or a lengthy essay in English – but it is vital to offer pupils useful feedback to improve. Of course, writing assessment is valuable to evaluate the impact of teachers' writing instruction.

Teachers can quickly become familiar with model writing, detailed rubrics, and comparisons between pupils' efforts, but making accurate judgements remains difficult. It takes time, training, and a strong understanding of the familiar expectations of a given genre, task, or audience.

In real terms, teachers' assessment of writing does not exist in a vacuum. National assessments – their criteria and exemplars – can drive writing practices. Exam grade descriptors can take on a magnitude that far outweighs their substance. Primary teacher assessment frameworks can signal the near-mythic significance of semi-colons, or spark endless debates about what is an allowable 'particular weakness'[1] for pupils' writing.

If we are not careful, writing tasks – along with assessment and feedback – can wither to little more than a pale imitation of exam writing.

It is useful to mark out the different purposes for writing assessment. Some writing is undertaken for national assessments, be that the real thing or mock practice. Similarly, teachers may want to establish a rank order for summative purposes. These approaches may offer an 'early warning' system for diagnosing struggling writers, or inform grouping decisions and similar. Ultimately, they should be undertaken sparingly.

Most writing undertaken in the classroom should not carry such high stakes. Formative, low stakes assessment should dominate our focus for writing instruction. This writing undertaken in the classroom is likely slower, stuffed full of explicit instruction, paying attention to the writing process – intentionally overlearning how to plan, compose sentences, revise, edit, revise again, and more.

A crucial consideration for teachers, and school leaders, is how to assess writing and when to address it in the curriculum. In primary school, the national curriculum offers a skeletal outline, but for many secondary school teachers, this is a blank slate. In secondary school, we can establish baselines that characterise handwriting, spelling, or planning strategies in general terms across subjects, but questions about writing development quickly become subject specific. Sensible approaches include building up features of academic writing through Key Stage 3, alongside seizing opportunities for vocabulary development that is sensitive to the curriculum, whilst being useful, and practised, in writing.

Writing assessment rubrics attempt to separate out the different moves in the big chess game of writing across a range of subject disciplines. As such, they can be useful starting points for teachers at all phases and for an array of writing tasks. For example, the Writing Assessment Measure (WAM)[2] for narrative writing, where pupils write for 15 minutes based on a writing prompt, breaks down the assessment into the following components:

- Handwriting (consistent, legible, and fluent)
- Spelling (correct spelling of complex vocabulary, including irregular words)
- Punctuation (a range of punctuation to clarify structure and create effect)
- Sentence structure and grammar (secure control of complex sentences)
- Vocabulary (powerful, well-chosen word choices)
- Organisation and overall structure (well-organised and cohesive writing)
- Ideas (interesting and creative ideas that engage the audience)

These moves are commonly identified in writing rubrics across a range of tasks, genres, and subject disciplines.

Even with well-structured rubrics that break down the writing moves we want pupils to develop, we should be wary of natural biases. Research has shown that well-written essays that have a high rate of spelling and grammar errors are judged more harshly.[3] It may be the case that the cosmetic, surface features of writing can sometimes trump the quality of the actual content of pupils' writing.

In secondary schools, spelling, punctuation and grammar are typically conflated and handwriting is politely ignored, given most secondary teachers would be flummoxed given the expectation to assess it. Of course, in many subject disciplines, writing can prove a vehicle for pupils to exhibit their knowledge. In a quiz in chemistry, or note-making in food and nutrition, it may be the case that the style, structure and accuracy is largely ignored, and the knowledge exhibited by pupils – their ideas, arguments, and the language they use – dominates what is assessed.

It should give us pause to consider the purpose of the writing assessment: are we assessing a pupils' background knowledge, their writing ability, or a combination of both?

A long-standing approach that can prove useful for teachers (and for pupils' peer assessment[4]) is reliably assessing pupils' writing using 'comparative judgement'. This describes the practice of comparing two pieces of writing and judging the better piece of writing. When you compare multiple pieces, ideally aggregating the judgements of multiple teachers, you can generate a reliable measurement scale. Not only that, you can also focus on lots of examples of writing, rather than an abstract notion of 'good writing'. It has led organisations like No More Marking to devise national online platforms for comparative judgement that have generated large national samples of comparable writing and very useful insights for teachers.

The simple notion of comparing two or more pieces of writing is familiar to teachers. It can of course offer insights into pupils' strengths and weaknesses that could prove more useful than being pinned to the often-troublesome criteria in a writing rubric. Daisy Christodoulou has written about how exam board descriptors for GCSE English Language can be tricky to interpret and apply:

> It is already not hard to see the kinds of problems such descriptors can cause. What is the difference between 'compelling' and 'highly engaging'? Or between 'effective' use of structural features and 'inventive' use?
>
> *Comparative judgement: The next big revolution in assessment?*,
> by Daisy Christodoulou[5]

In my past, I have spent time painstakingly analysing the wording of examination rubrics and then converting them to 'pupil friendly' language. Too often, pupils would struggle to interpret their meaning regardless of seemingly 'friendly' terminology, but then when I would share worked examples, or model exemplar writing myself, they would be able to better characterise the expectations of the task in concrete terms. We needn't rule out all rubrics, but we should take great care in overusing them – particularly with our novice writers.

We can support teachers to undertake more targeted, narrow, and precise writing assessments. For example, teachers who want to assess pupils' handwriting can use the Handwriting Legibility Scale[6] (find it here: https://bit.ly/3Cgpq31), or you could use handy handwriting speed rules of thumb based on words written per minute (WPM),[7] such as:

Age	WPM
9	10
10	12
11	14
12	16
13	18
14	20
15	22
16	24

We can recognise that a range of factors could influence handwriting fluency and legibility (alongside typing speed). For instance, copying from a text is an easier task to manage compared to having the extra demand of generating your own ideas and vocabulary. Also, if pupils have a high level of background knowledge of a given topic, and/or the text type being undertaken, they can generate their ideas more quickly which speeds up their handwriting.[8]

When we consider assessing whole class writing, it may be that we don't try to assess everything equally, but instead we target a writing move we have just taught explicitly. For instance, a common issue is pupils failing to revise and edit their writing in depth. Often, this is a case of them not having strategies to do so (e.g. using a checklist, considering the viewpoint of their audience, or revising vocabulary choices). We can target our assessment to judge the number, and quality, of revisions and edits a pupil has undertaken, either for a single writing task, or in their prep book more broadly. Monitoring a small number of moves for a given writing task can generate simpler feedback for pupils to manage, whilst helping mitigate teacher workload too.

Put simply, assessing individual components of writing – such as handwriting, spelling, vocabulary use, the extent of pupils' editing, or sentence-level writing – is limited in scope, but can prove useful to teachers and meaningful for novice pupils. Insights from such diagnostic assessments can help us adapt teaching, or retrain pupils on editing strategies and more.

Teachers can seek out useful assessment tools for writing that explore areas beyond SPaG and exam assessments. Researchers have developed an assessment tool to try to measure pupils' writing self-efficacy (that is to say, a pupil's confidence in their ability to write well). With their Self-efficacy for Writing Scale (SEWS),[9] they propose three areas:

- **Ideation**: pupils' confidence in their ability to generate ideas for their writing.
- **Conventions**: pupils' confidence in their ability to follow conventions of grammar, punctuation, and spelling.
- **Self-regulation**: pupils' confidence in their ability to stay focused on their writing task, manage their emotions and persevere through challenges.

It is easy to recognise the value of understanding how much confidence, and enjoyment, pupils experience when they write. The match between being good at something and being self-confident is obviously important, but by exploring pupils' attitudes to writing we can complement our understanding of their writing moves.

Paying attention to pupils' will and skill is likely to offer us a richer picture so we can both assess and address writing successfully. Writing is a complex act. We cannot assess the chess game with one assessment move, but we can make a meaningful start.

Focusing on feedback

For centuries, feedback on pupils' writing has typically been narrowly focused on correction of seeming errors, rather than appraising effectiveness and developing a broad range of writing moves. The tyrannical reign of the red pen has left an enduring stain.

A narrow focus on correcting errors is likely to only skim the surface of the plethora of writing moves a pupil needs to enact most writing tasks. Meeting the standard of accurate academic writing no doubt has value, but we shouldn't obsess over errors just because they are easily observable.

Indeed, in special cases, an error may even profit our pupils! The 'Wicked Bible', a 400-year-old bible that omitted the word 'not' from the commandment 'Thou shalt [not] commit adultery' was subsequently sold for £31,250 in London, in 2015. It is highly unlikely that advice to 'make mistakes and get rich' proves helpful in the classroom, but we should be careful not to obsess over minor errors.

Teachers often consider the best methods for feedback on pupils' writing. Is verbal or written feedback the best? The evidence on this question appears to be equivocal. Instead, when you dig into the evidence on feedback, applying careful principles to feeding back on writing trumps whether the form is written or offered verbally.[10] Equally, whether grades or marks are assigned to the writing or whether written feedback on writing is daubed in green or red pen matters very little.

The Education Endowment Foundation's guidance report *Teacher feedback to improve pupil learning*[11] explains that 'personal' feedback (such as 'brilliant work – you're a natural, gifted writer') is less likely to prove effective than feedback on writing that addresses the task, the subject, and self-regulation strategies:

	Task	Subject	Self-regulation
Feedback on writing	Year 5 pupils have been writing an argument about crime and punishment, but their arguments have proven thin on examples. Whole class feedback targets modelling paragraphs including multiple examples of crime and punishment from different eras in history.	In year 9 religious education, a group of pupils who have written explanations of attitudes to ethical debates, such as marriage and divorce, are directed to refer more specifically to evidence derived from sacred texts.	In year 12, pupils from an English Literature class are receiving feedback on their poetry essays. They are given feedback on the number and quality of their revisions and edits. The teacher then discusses their time taken on revising and editing, along with exploring strategies they employed to do this.

Table inspired by and adapted from the EEF guidance report *Teacher feedback to improve pupil learning*

The debate about methods of feedback – verbal or written – often ignores the complex truth that feedback on writing is invariably a complex hybrid of the two methods. Writing is so challenging for novice pupils that they need as much support and reinforcement as possible. An added complication is that pupils can find teacher's written feedback to be 'enigmatic',[12] so additional dialogue to explain any written feedback is usually necessary if we want pupils to reflect and revise their writing successfully.

Writer and Oxford don Arthur Quiller-Couch once famously stated that as a writer you have to 'murder your darlings' when editing and revising your own writing. Around a century later, superstar novelist Stephen King added an essential update: 'It's always easier to kill someone else's darlings than toil on your own.'[13]

What might this mean for our pupils?

It is not enough that teachers offer pupils feedback; pupils need to assess their own writing performance. And yet, as King captured, being objective and reflective about your own writing is difficult. It may be that peer feedback offers a crucial prerequisite for any effective self-assessment undertaken by pupils.[14] Given the crucial importance of pupils developing a strong awareness of the audience for their writing, pupils offering an audience for one another can prove a timely boon.

If teachers are activating pupils to offer feedback to one another, then the precision of that feedback needs explicit modelling. We return once more to pupils being able to precisely identify the range of writing moves for a given task and subject domain.

The benefits of well-structured peer tutoring, and being an authentic editor (taking on the role of the notional audience of the text), seems to be as impactful for the pupil who is tasked with editing as it is for the pupil receiving the feedback and edits on their writing. When it comes to writing, it helps to see the model responses of others, given it can help cohere your thinking about the task at hand, offering a refined understanding that you can bring back to editing and revising your own efforts.

What is clear is that it requires time and effort to develop pupil knowledge and writing skill, so that the time invested in feedback is meaningful, whether it is undertaken by the teacher, peers, or by oneself.

The transformative power of writing

Writing both creates and changes history.

Creative acts of writing shape our sense of who we are, offering us historical milestones and personal touchstones.

Writing marks out profound historical breakthroughs, from the Rosetta Stone to the first internet protocol, from Shakespeare composing his first play to Martin Luther King offering up his dreams in the greatest of speeches. These singular moments in our history can seem monumental and distant from our lived experience in the classroom. And yet, they all inevitably share the same humble origins: each author learned to write in a classroom.

What connects all these great writers and thinkers who changed our world are their unheralded teachers; the teachers who made gentle but indelible marks on their thinking, so that they could change the world, and themselves, in the act of writing. It is a truly remarkable legacy that is within the grasp of every teacher reading this book.

There is a thin, near imperceptible line to be traced from a sentence written in a pupil's schoolbook to the potential of their future. It may be the potential of workaday notes in a science book that ends in the discovery of a new vaccine decades later, or the copycat purple prose written in year 8 English that proves the seed of a global bestseller. Most of this writing will not make the history books, of course, but it will help shape the story of our pupils' lives. I cannot think of anything more important to positively influence for a teacher.

Closing the writing gap then is the story of countless small acts of effortful practice. Such an act may seem insignificant on the surface. It is Jamila revising a tricky sentence three times over. It is James compiling his vocabulary inventory. It is Zara planning and replanning her history essay. It is Tom reading and re-reading his geography case study. It is Rosie researching evidence for her balanced argument. It is Adil editing his art portfolio prose. It is Emma plotting her first detective story.

And yet, each small daily act of writing accumulates into something bigger. Over time, writing skill goes on to circumscribe or provide a platform for school success. From infant mark making to older students mastering essays in the exam hall, we can see how much writing matters.

And so, let's return to those crucial seven steps that can help us begin to close the writing gap:

1. Train teachers in the art and science of writing.
2. Take advantage of talk and the rhetorical roots of writing.
3. Explicitly teach and model the stages of the writing process.
4. Offer pupils the gift of grammar, so that they can make informed writing choices.
5. Concentrate on crafting great sentences.
6. Prioritise disciplinary writing.
7. Plan for focused feedback and assess writing excellence.

Thank you for reading this book, and for making your mark so that your pupils may make their own.

Notes

1 MacNeill, S. (2018). A very particular weakness. Herts for Learning, 2018 February 21. Retrieved from: www.hertsforlearning.co.uk/blog/very-particular-weakness.
2 Dunsmuir et al. (2015). An evaluation of the Writing Assessment Measure (WAM) for children's narrative writing. *Assessing Writing, 23,* 1–18.
3 Rezaei, A. R., & Lovorn, M. (2010). Reliability and validity of rubrics for assessment through writing. *Assessing Writing, 15,* 18–39. https://doi.org/10.1016/j.asw.2010.01.003.
4 Jones, I., & Wheadon, C. (2015). Peer assessment using comparative and absolute judgement. *Studies in Educational Evaluation, 47,* 93–101.
5 Christodoulou, D. (2018). Comparative judgement: The next big revolution in assessment? Retrieved from: https://researched.org.uk/2018/07/06/comparative-judgement-the-next-big-revolution-in-assessment-2/.
6 Barnett, A. L., Prunty, M., & Rosenblum, S. (2018). Development of the Handwriting Legibility Scale (HLS): a preliminary examination of Reliability and Validity. *Research in Developmental Disabilities, 72,* 240–247.
7 Murphy-Francis, D. (2016). Handwriting assessment for teachers and parents. Retrieved from: https://educational-psychologist.co.uk/sen-resources-blog/2016/1/22/handwriting-assessment-for-teachers-and-parents.
8 Willingham, D. (2006). How knowledge helps. *American Educator,* Spring 2006. Accessed online at: www.aft.org/periodical/american-educator/spring-2006/how-knowledge-helps.
9 Bruning et al. (2013). Examining dimensions for self-efficacy for writing. *Journal of Educational Psychology, 105*(1), 25–38. Accessed online at: www.researchgate.net/publication/258111166_Examining_Dimensions_of_Self-Efficacy_for_Writing/link/02e7e526fe5d8e5b34000000/download.

10 Education Endowment Foundation. (2021). *Teacher feedback to improve pupil learning.* London: Education Endowment Foundation.
11 Ibid.
12 Allen, L., Roscoe, R., & McNamara, D. (2013). Evaluative misalignment of 10th-grade student and teacher criteria for essay quality: An automated textual analysis. *Journal of Writing Research, 5*, 35–59. 10.17239/jowr-2013.05.01.2.
13 King, S. (2012). *On writing: A memoir of the craft.* New York: Simon & Schuster.
14 Black, P., Harrison, C., Lee, C., Marshall, B., & William, D. (2003). *Assessment for learning – putting it into practice.* Maidenhead: Open University Press.

Appendix: Glossary of terms

Rhetorical devices

Anadiplosis – A type of repetition in which the last word of one clause or sentence is repeated as the first word of the following clause or sentence.

Anaphora – A type of repetition which repeats a sequence of words or phrases at the beginnings of sentences or clauses.

Anastrophe – A structural device that changes the typical word order of a sentence for emphasis ('Yoda sentences').

Antithesis – A structural device that places two opposite ideas together in a sentence or sentences.

Asyndeton – A device which has a strong rhythmic pattern, but that omits conjunctions (such as 'and' or 'but').

Chiasmus – A structural device that takes the structure of two phrases or sentences, with the second part of the sentence structure being reversed, creating balance and symmetry.

Epistrophe – A type of repetition that repeats a sequence of words or phrases at the ends of sentences or clauses.

Eutrepismus – A structural device that organises clauses or sentences numerically or in an ordered sequence for clarity.

Ethos – An appeal to the writer's own character.

Logos – An appeal to reason.

Pathos – An appeal to emotions and beliefs.

Polysyndeton – A device which has a strong rhythmic pattern that intentionally repeats conjunctions for added rhythmic effect.

Progymnasmata – A fourteen-step series of writing exercises from ancient Rome.

Tricolon – A structural device that creates a series of three words, phrases or sentences that are parallel in structure, length or rhythm.

Grammar and writing

Adjective – A word that describes the attributes of a noun, e.g. 'blue', 'smart', 'tricky'.

Adverb – A word or phrase that modifies or qualifies a verb, an adjective, or other adverbs (often ending in -ly), e.g. 'angrily', 'quietly', 'hungrily'.

Fronted adverbial – When the adverb (a word or phrase) moves to the front of the sentence, before the verb, e.g. 'Firstly,...' and 'Earlier today...'.

Clauses

Appositive clause – A noun phrase that is placed next to another noun to explain it or identify it more precisely, e.g. 'The girl, *an avid reader and writer,* quickly completed the tale.'

Dependent clause – A clause that cannot stand alone as a complete sentence, e.g. 'which was important to the class'.

Embedded clause – A clause used in the middle of another clause, e.g. 'My class, *who are enthusiastic writers*, began their new project'.

Independent (main clause) – A clause that can stand alone as a complete sentence, e.g. 'The class wrote their balanced argument.'

Subordinate clause – A clause, most typically introduced by a conjunction, that is dependent upon the main clause.

Collocation – Words that appear frequently together in use, e.g. 'make do', or 'avid reader'.

Comma splice – The use of a comma to link two independent clauses instead of a conjunction, colon, or a semicolon.

Composition – How a writer assembles words and ideas into sentences.

End focused sentences – When longer noun phrases are placed at the end of the sentence and the final word, or words, retains a memorable emphasis.

Executive function – Our personal control centre that supports us to plan, sustain our attention, and stick to our goals when writing.

Fragment – An incomplete sentence that typically omits a subject or a verb, or both subject and verb, e.g. 'Because of the storm' [because of the storm what?]

Homophones – Two or more words having the same pronunciation but different meanings, or spelling, e.g. 'new' and 'knew'.

Nominalisation – The process of making a noun from a verb or adjective, e.g. 'sweat/perspire' > 'perspiration'.

Nouns/noun phrase – A word used to describe any class of people, places, or things (common nouns), or the name of a particular one of these (proper noun).

Passive voice (opposite = active voice) – The subject of the sentence is acted on by the verb, e.g. 'The solution was mixed in the beaker.'

Right branching sentences – The subject (noun) and the verb appear at the start of the sentence, for clarity, with additional details then branching off to the right of the sentence.

Subject verb agreement – The subject and the verb in the sentence agree in number, e.g. The clothes are too small for me' not 'The clothes is too small for me.'

Syntax – The arrangement of words, phrases, and clauses in sentences.

Transcription – The act of writing, including handwriting, accurate spelling, or typing.

Verbs

Auxiliary verb – A helping verb used to express the main verb's tense, mood, or voice, e.g. 'am', 'were', 'has', 'had', 'does', 'did'.

Modal verb – A helping verb that adds to the main verb by expressing possibility, ability, or permission, e.g. 'can', 'could', 'might', 'may', 'should'.

State verb – Describes the state of something (as opposed to an action verb). e.g. 'believe', 'imagine', 'dislike', 'belong', 'understand', and 'love'.

Bibliography

Ahmed, T., Kent, S., Cirino, P. T., & Keller-Margulis, M. (2021). The not-so-simple view of writing in struggling readers/writers. *Reading & Writing Quarterly*, doi:10.1080/10573569.2021.1948374.

Applebee, A. N. (2000). Alternative models of writing development. In R. Indrisano, & J. R. Squire (Eds.), *Perspectives on writing: Research, theory, and practice* (pp. 90–110). International Reading Association, doi:10.1598/0872072681.4.

Applebee, A. N., & Langer, J. A. (2009). What is happening in the teaching of writing? *English Journal, 98*(5) (2009), 18–38.

Applebee, A, N., Lehr, F., & Auten, A. (1981). Learning to write in the secondary school: How and where. *The English Journal, 70*(5), 78–82.

Barrs, M. (2019). Teaching bad writing. *English in Education, 53*(1), 18–31, doi:10.1080/04250494.2018.1557858.

Berninger, V. W., Nagy, W. E., & Beers, S. (2011). Child writers' construction and reconstruction of single sentences and construction of multi-sentence texts: contributions of syntax and transcription to translation. *Reading and Writing, 24*, 151–182.

Berninger, V., Vaughan, K., Abbott, R. D., Begay, K., Coleman, K.B., Curtin, G., ...Graham., S. (2002). Teaching spelling and composition alone and together: Implications for the simple view of writing. *Journal of Educational Psychology, 94*, 291–304, doi:10.1037/0022-0663.94.2.291.

Biber, D., & Gray, B. (2010). Challenging stereotypes about academic writing: Complexity, elaboration, explicitness. *Journal of English for Academic Purposes, 9*, 2–20.

Biber, D., & Gray, B. (2016). *Grammatical complexity in academic English.* Cambridge: Cambridge University Press.

Bibliography

Brown, A. (2018). *Understanding and teaching English spelling: A strategic guide.* Oxon: Routledge.

Bruning, R., Kauffman, D., Dempsey, M. S., & Zumbrunn, S. (2013). Examining dimensions of self-efficacy for writing. *Journal of Educational Psychology, 105*(1), 25–38.

Cabell, S. Q., Tortorelli, L. S., & Gerde, H. K. (2013). How do I write...? Scaffolding preschoolers' early writing skills. *The Reading Teacher, 66,* (8), 650–659.

Chang, W., & Ku, Y-M. (2015). The effects of note-taking skills instruction on elementary students' reading. *The Journal of Educational Research, 108*(4), 278–291, doi:10.1080/00220671.2014.886175.

Chen, H., Myhill, D., & Lewis, H. (2020). *Developing writers across the primary and secondary years: Growing into writing.* Oxon: Routledge.

Christodoulou, D. (2016). *Making good progress? The future of assessment for learning.* Oxon: Routledge.

Coffin, C. (2006). Learning the language of school history: the role of linguistics in mapping the writing demands of the secondary school curriculum. *Journal of Curriculum Studies, 38*(4), 413–429.

Crystal, D. (2007). *Words, words, words.* USA: Oxford University Press.

Crystal, D. (2012). *Spell it out: the singular story of English spelling.* London: Profile Books.

Crystal, D. (2015). *Making a point: The pernickety story of English punctuation.* London: Profile Books.

Crystal, D. (2017). *Making sense: The glamorous story of English grammar.* London: Profile Books.

Didau, D. (2021). *Making meaning in English: Exploring the role of knowledge in the English curriculum.* Oxon: Routledge.

Drew, S. V. et al. (2017). Framework for Disciplinary Writing in Science Grades 6–12: A National Survey. *Journal of Educational Psychology, 109*(7), 935–955.

Dombey, H. (2013). What we know about teaching writing. *Preschool and Primary Education, 1*(1), 22–40.

Dockrell, J. E., Marshall, C. R., & Wyse, D. (2016). Teachers' reported practices for teaching writing in England. *Reading and Writing, 29,* 409–434. doi:10.1007/s11145-015-9605-9.

Dunsmuir et al. (2014). An evaluation of the Writing Assessment Measure (WAM) for children's narrative writing. *Assessing Writing 23,* 1–18.

Education Endowment Foundation. (2018). *Metacognition and self-regulation guidance report.* London: Education Endowment Foundation.

Education Endowment Foundation. (2018). *Preparing for literacy: Improving communication, language and literacy in the early years guidance report.* London: Education Endowment Foundation.

Education Endowment Foundation. (2019). *Improving literacy in secondary schools guidance report*. London: Education Endowment Foundation.

Education Endowment Foundation. (2021). *Improving literacy in key stage 1*. London: Education Endowment Foundation.

Education Endowment Foundation. (2021). *Improving literacy in key stage 2*. London: Education Endowment Foundation.

Education Endowment Foundation. (2021). *Teacher feedback to improve pupil learning*. London: Education Endowment Foundation.

Enderle, P. et al. (2013). Cross-disciplinary writing: Scientific argumentation, the common core, and the ADI model. *Science Scope, 37*(1), 16–22.

Eunice Kennedy Shriver National Institute of Child Health and Human Development, NIH, DHHS. (2010). *What content-area teachers should know about adolescent literacy (NA)*. Washington, DC: US Government Printing Office.

Feng, L., Joshi, R. M. M., Lindner, A., & Ji, X. R. (2019). The roles of handwriting and keyboarding in writing: A meta-analytic review. *Reading and Writing, 32*(1). doi:10.1007/s11145-017-9749-x.

Fischer, S. R. (2003). *A history of writing*. Netherlands: Reaktion Books Ltd.

Fish, S. (2012). *How to write a sentence and how to read one*. New York: Harper Paperbacks.

Fletcher-Wood, H. (2021). *Habits of success: Getting every student learning*. Oxon: Routledge.

Gathercole, S. E., & Alloway, T. P. (2007). *Understanding Working Memory: A Classroom Guide*. Working Memory & Learning. London: Harcourt Assessment.

Gibbons, P. (2015). *Scaffolding language, scaffolding learning: Teaching English language learners in the mainstream classroom* (2nd ed.). Portsmouth: Heinemann.

Graham, S. (1999). Handwriting and spelling instruction for students with learning disabilities: A review. *Learning Disability Quarterly, 22*(2), 78–98.

Graham, S. (2011). The process writing approach: A meta-analysis. *The Journal of Educational Research, 104*, 396–407.

Graham, S. (2018). Handwriting instruction: a commentary on five studies. *Reading and Writing, 31*(4), 1–11. doi:10.1007/s11145-018-9854-5.

Graham, S. (2020). The sciences of reading and writing must become more fully integrated. *Reading Research Quarterly, 55*(S1), s35–s44.

Graham, S., & Hebert, M. (2011). Writing to read: A meta-analysis of the impact of writing and writing instruction on reading.

Harvard Educational Review, 81, 710–744. 10.17763/haer.81.4.t2kom13756113566.

Graham, S., & Hebert, M. A. (2010). *Writing to read: Evidence for how writing can improve reading. A Carnegie Corporation Time to Act Report.* Washington, DC: Alliance for Excellent Education.

Graham, S., Liu, X., Aitken, A., Ng, C., Bartlett, B., Harris, K., & Holzapfel, J. (2017). Effectiveness of literacy programs balancing reading and writing instruction: A meta-analysis. *Reading Research Quarterly, 53*(3), 279–304. doi:10.1002/rrq.194.

Graham, S., MacArthur, C. A., & Hebert, M. (2019). *Best practices in writing instruction.* London: The Guilford Press.

Graham, S., & Perin, D. (2007). *Writing next: Effective strategies to improve writing of adolescents in middle and high schools – A report to Carnegie Corporation of New York.* Washington, DC: Alliance for Excellent Education.

Graham, S., & Rijlaarsdam, G. (2016). Writing education around the globe: introduction and call for a new global analysis. *Reading and Writing, 29*, 781–792.

Grigorenko, E. L., Mambrino, E., & Preiss, D. D. (2012). *Writing: A mosaic of new perspectives.* Hove: Psychology Press.

Halliday, M. A. K. (2004a). The grammatical construction of scientific knowledge: The framing of the English clause. In Webster, J. J. (Ed.), *The language of science* (Volume 5 in the Collected Works of M. A. K. Halliday) (pp. 102–134). London: Continuum.

Halliday, M. A. K., & Matthiessen (2004b). *An Introduction to Functional Grammar* (3rd ed.). London: Hodder Arnold.

Harmey, S., & Wilkinson, I. (2019). A critical review of the logics of inquiry in studies of early writing development. *Journal of Writing Research, 11*(1), 41–78.

Harris, K. R., & Graham, S. (2016). Self-regulated strategy development in writing: Policy implications of an evidence-based practice. *Policy Insights from the Behavioural and Brain Sciences, 3*(1), 77–84.

Harris, K., R., Graham, S., Mason, L., H., & Saddler, B. (2002). Developing self-regulated writers. *Theory Into Practice, 41*(2), 110–115. doi:10.1207/s15430421tip4102_7.

Hattan, C., & Lupo, S. M. (2020). Rethinking the role of knowledge in the literacy classroom. *Reading Research Quarterly, 55*(S1), S283–S298.

Heller, R., & Greenleaf, C. L. (2007). *Literacy instruction in the content areas: getting to the core of middle and high school improvement.* Washington, DC: Alliance for Excellent Education.

Hinkel, E. (2020). *Teaching academic L2 writing: Practical techniques in vocabulary and grammar.* Oxon: Routledge.

Hochman, J. C., & Wexler, N. (2017). *The writing revolution: A guide to adapting thinking through writing in all subjects and grades.* San Francisco, CA: Jossey-Bass.

Hodgson, J., & Harris, A. (2021) Make grammar great again? *English in Education, 55*(3), 208–221. doi:10.1080/04250494.2021.1943225.

Hughes, E. M., & Lee, J.-Y. (2020). Effects of a mathematical writing intervention on middle school students' performance. *Reading & Writing Quarterly, 36*(2), 176–192. doi:10.1080/10573569.2019.1677537.

Hunter, K., & Tse, H. (2013). Making disciplinary writing and thinking practices an integral part of academic content teaching. *Active Learning in Higher Education, 14*(3), 227–239. doi:10.1177/1469787413498037.

Jones, I., & Wheadon, C. (2015). Peer assessment using comparative and absolute judgement. *Studies in Educational Evaluation, 47*, 93–101.

Kellogg, R. T. (2008). Training writing skills: A cognitive developmental perspective. *Journal of Writing Research, 1*(1), 1–26.

Kennedy, G. A. (2013). *Quintilian: A Roman educator and his quest for the perfect orator.* Sophron.

King, S. (2012). *On writing: A memoir of the craft.* New York: Simon & Schuster.

Lampi, J. P., & Reynolds, T. (2018). Connecting practice and research: From tacit to explicit disciplinary writing instruction. *Journal of Developmental Education, 41*(2).

Lee, C. C. (2007). Graphic organisers as scaffolding for students' revision in the pre-writing stage. In *ICT: Providing choices for learners and learning.* Proceedings ascilite Singapore 2007. www.ascilite.org.au/conferences/singapore07/procs/lee-cc.pdf.

Leith, S. (2017). *Write to the point.* London: Profile Books Ltd.

Leith, S. (2011). *You talkin' to me? Rhetoric from Aristotle to Obama.* London: Profile Books Ltd.

MacArthur, C. A., Graham, S., & Fitzgerald, J. (2017). *Handbook of writing research.* New York: The Guilford Press.

McCutchen, D. (2011). From novice to expert: Implications of language skills and relevant knowledge for memory during the development of writing skill. *Journal of Writing Research, 2*(1), 51–68.

Mason, L. H., Harris, K. R., & Graham, S. (2011). Self-regulated strategy development for students with writing difficulties. *Theory into Practice, 50*(1), 20–27. doi:10.1080/00405841.2011.534922.

McGhee, M. W., & Lew, C. (2007). Leadership and writing: How principals' knowledge, beliefs, and interventions affect writing instruction in elementary and secondary schools. *Educational Administration Quarterly, 43*(3) 358–380.

Moran, J. (2018). *First you write a sentence.* London: Penguin Books.

Myhill, D. (2000). Misconceptions and difficulties in the acquisition of metalinguistic knowledge. *Language and Education, 14*(3), 151–163. doi:10.1080/09500780008666787.

Myhill, D. (2001). Writing: crafting and creating. *English in Education, 35*(3), 13–20. doi:10.1111/j.1754-8845.2001.tb00744.x.

Myhill, D. (2005). Testing times: the impact of prior knowledge on written genres produced in examination settings. *Assessment in Education: Principles, Policy & Practice, 12*(3), 289–300. doi:10.1080/09695940500337256.

Myhill, D., Jones, S., & Watson, A. (2012). Grammar matters: How teachers' grammatical knowledge impacts on the teaching of writing. *Teaching and Teacher Education, 36*, 77–91.

Murphy, J. J. (2012). *A short history of writing instruction: From Ancient Greece to contemporary America* (3rd ed.). New York: Routledge.

Murphy, J. J., & Wiese, C. (2016). *Quintilian: On the teaching of speaking and writing* (2nd ed.). Carbondale, IL: Southern Illinois University Press.

Nagy, W., & Townsend, D. (2012). Words as tools: Learning academic vocabulary as language acquisition. *Reading Research Quarterly, 47*(1), 91–108.

Neuen, S., & Tebeaux, E. (2017). *Writing science right: Strategies for teaching scientific writing.* Oxon: Routledge.

Peacock, C. (2019). *Teaching writing: A systematic approach.* Oxon: Routledge.

Petelin, R. (2016). *How writing works: A field guide to effective writing.* Oxon: Routledge.

Quigley, A. (2018). *Closing the vocabulary gap.* Oxon: Routledge.

Quigley, A. (2020). *Closing the reading gap.* Oxon: Routledge.

Rastle, K. (2019). EPS mid-career prize lecture: Writing systems, reading and language. *The Quarterly Journal of Experimental Psychology, 72(4)*, 677–692. https://doi.org/10.1177/1747021819829696.

Reed, D. (2012). *Why teach spelling?* Portsmouth, NH: RMC Research Corporation, Centre on Instruction.

Schwellnus, H., Cameron, H., & Carnahan, H. (2012). Which to choose? Manuscript or cursive handwriting? A review of the literature. *Journal of Occupational Therapy, Schools, & Early Intervention, 5*(3–4).

Shanahan, C. (2015). *Disciplinary literacy strategies in content area classes.* International Literacy Association Essentials.

Shanahan, T., & Shanahan, C. (2017). Disciplinary Literacy: Just the FAQs. *Educational Leadership: Journal of the Department of Supervision and Curriculum Development, N.E.A., 74*(5), 18–22.

Shanahan, T., & Shanahan, C. (2008). Teaching disciplinary literacy to adolescents: Rethinking content-area literacy. *Harvard Educational Review, 78*(1), 40–59.

Shanahan, C., & Shanahan, T. (2014). The implications of disciplinary literacy. *Journal of Adolescent and Adult Literacy, 57*(8), 628–631.

Sumner, E., Barnett, A. L., & Connelly, V. (2014). The influence of spelling ability on handwriting production: Children with and without dyslexia. *Journal of Experimental Psychology: Learning, Memory and Cognition, 40*(5), 1441–1447.

Teng, M. F. (2020). Young learners' reading and writing performance: Exploring collaborative modelling of text structure as an additional component of self-regulated strategy development. *Studies in Educational Evaluation, 65*, 100870.

Truss, L. (2009). *Eats, shoots & leaves: The zero-tolerance approach to punctuation.* London: Fourth Estate.

Van der Schaaf, M., Baartman, L., Prins, F., Oosterbaan, A., & Schaap, H. (2013). Feedback dialogues that stimulate students' reflective thinking. *Scandinavian Journal of Educational Research, 57*(3), 227–245.

Watanabe, L. M., & Hall-Kenyon, K. M. (2011). Improving young children's writing: The influence of story structure on kindergartners' writing complexity. *Literacy Research and Instruction, 50*(4), 272–293. doi:10.1080/19388071.2010.514035.

Watson, C. (2019). *Semicolon.* London: Fourth Estate.

Wexler, N. (2019). *The knowledge gap: The hidden cause of America's broken education system – and how to fix it.* New York: Avery.

Wyse, D. (2017). *How writing works: From the invention of the alphabet to the rise of social media.* Cambridge: Cambridge University Press.

Index

Note: page numbers in *italic* type refer to Figures. As 'writing' is the major subject of this title, entries under this keyword have been kept to a minimum, and readers are advised to seek more specific headings.

Index

Index

www.ingramcontent.com/pod-product-compliance
Lightning Source LLC
LaVergne TN
LVHW010901110826
845149LV00005B/1434

* 9 7 8 1 0 3 2 0 1 7 7 1 6 *